J970.3 HOPI

j973.049 Bonvillain, Nancy.
B
        The Hopi.

$19.95

DATE			

THE
HOPI

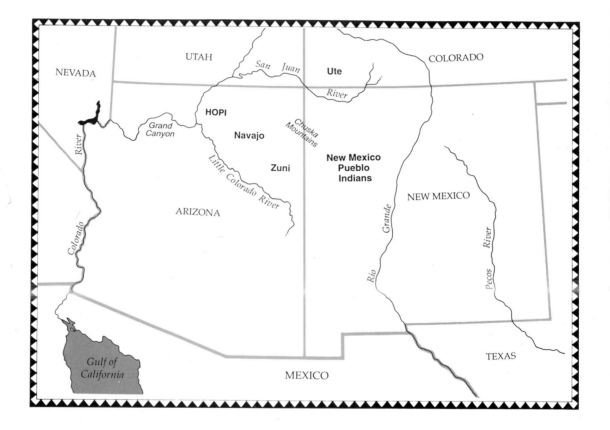

INDIANS OF NORTH AMERICA

THE
HOPI

Nancy Bonvillain
New School for Social Research

Frank W. Porter III
General Editor

CHELSEA HOUSE PUBLISHERS
New York   Philadelphia

On the cover   A Hopi doll representing the kachina known as Na'nga sohu, or chasing star.

Chelsea House Publishers
Editorial Director   Richard Rennert
Executive Managing Editor   Karyn Gullen Browne
Copy Chief   Robin James
Picture Editor   Adrian G. Allen
Art Director   Robert Mitchell
Manufacturing Director   Gerald Levine
Production Coordinator   Marie Claire Cebrían-Ume

Indians of North America
Senior Editor   Sean Dolan

Staff for **THE HOPI**
Associate Editor   David Carter
Editorial Assistant   Annie McDonnell
Senior Designer   Rae Grant
Picture Researcher   Alan Gottlieb

5   7   9   8   6   4

Library of Congress Cataloging-in-Publication Data

Bonvillain, Nancy.
    The Hopi / Nancy Bonvillain; Frank W. Porter III, general editor.
        p.   cm.—(Indians of North America)
    Includes bibliographical references and index.
    ISBN 0-7910-1682-X.—0-7910-0725-1 (pbk.)
    1. Hopi Indians—History—Juvenile literature. 2. Hopi Indians—Social life and customs—Juvenile literature.
[1. Hopi Indians.   2. Indians of North America.]   I. Porter, Frank W., 1947–   .   II. Series: Indians of North America (Chelsea House Publishers)
E99.H7B66   1994   93-11978
973'.04974—dc20   CIP
                                                          AC

CONTENTS

INDIANS OF NORTH AMERICA

CHELSEA HOUSE PUBLISHERS

INDIANS OF NORTH AMERICA: CONFLICT AND SURVIVAL

Frank W. Porter III

The Indians survived our open intention of wiping them out, and since the tide turned they have even weathered our good intentions toward them, which can be much more deadly.

John Steinbeck
America and Americans

When Europeans first reached the North American continent, they found hundreds of tribes occupying a vast and rich country. The newcomers quickly recognized the wealth of natural resources. They were not, however, so quick or willing to recognize the spiritual, cultural, and intellectual riches of the people they called Indians.

The Indians of North America examines the problems that develop when people with different cultures come together. For American Indians, the consequences of their interaction with non-Indian people have been both productive and tragic. The Europeans believed they had "discovered" a "New World," but their religious bigotry, cultural bias, and materialistic world view kept them from appreciating and understanding the people who lived in it. All too often they attempted to change the way of life of the indigenous people. The Spanish conquistadores wanted the Indians as a source of labor. The Christian missionaries, many of whom were English, viewed them as potential converts. French traders and trappers used the Indians as a means to obtain pelts. As Francis Parkman, the 19th-century historian, stated, "Spanish civilization crushed the Indian; English civilization scorned and neglected him; French civilization embraced and cherished him."

Nearly 500 years later, many people think of American Indians as curious vestiges of a distant past, waging a futile war to survive in a Space Age society. Even today, our understanding of the history and culture of American Indians is too often derived from unsympathetic, culturally biased, and inaccurate reports. The American Indian, described and portrayed in thousands of movies, television programs, books, articles, and government studies, has either been raised to the status of the "noble savage" or disparaged as the "wild Indian" who resisted the westward expansion of the American frontier.

Where in this popular view are the real Indians, the human beings and communities whose ancestors can be traced back to ice-age hunters? Where are the creative and indomitable people whose sophisticated technologies used the natural resources to ensure their survival, whose military skill might even have prevented European settlement of North America if not for devastating epidemics and disruption of the ecology? Where are the men and women who are today diligently struggling to assert their legal rights and express once again the value of their heritage?

The various Indian tribes of North America, like people everywhere, have a history that includes population expansion, adaptation to a range of regional environments, trade across wide networks, internal strife, and warfare. This was the reality. Europeans justified their conquests, however, by creating a mythical image of the New World and its native people. In this myth, the New World was a virgin land, waiting for the Europeans. The arrival of Christopher Columbus ended a timeless primitiveness for the original inhabitants.

Also part of this myth was the debate over the origins of the American Indians. Fantastic and diverse answers were proposed by the early explorers, missionairies, and settlers. Some thought that the Indians were descended from the Ten Lost Tribes of Israel, others that they were descended from inhabitants of the lost continent of Atlantis. One writer suggested that the Indians had reached North America in another Noah's ark.

A later myth, perpetrated by many historians, focused on the relentless persecution during the past five centuries until only a scattering of these "primitive" people remained to be herded onto reservations. This view fails to chronicle the overt and covert ways in which the Indians successfully coped with the intruders.

All of these myths presented one-sided interpretations that ignored the complexity of European and American events and policies. All left serious questions unanswered. What were the origins of the American Indians? Where did they come from? How and when did they get to the New World? What was their life—their culture—really like?

In the late 1800s, anthropologists and archaeologists in the Smithsonian Institution's newly created Bureau of American Ethnology in Washington,

D.C., began to study scientifically the history and culture of the Indians of North America. They were motivated by an honest belief that the Indians were on the verge of extinction and that along with them would vanish their languages, religious beliefs, technology, myths, and legends. These men and women went out to visit, study, and record data from as many Indian communities as possible before this information was forever lost.

By this time there was a new myth in the national consciousness. American Indians existed as figures in the American past. They had performed a historical mission. They had challenged white settlers who trekked across the continent. Once conquered, however, they were supposed to accept graciously the way of life of their conquerors.

The reality again was different. American Indians resisted both actively and passively. They refused to lose their unique identity, to be assimilated into white society. Many whites viewed the Indians not only as members of a conquered nation but also as "inferior" and "unequal." The rights of the Indians could be expanded, contracted, or modified as the conquerors saw fit. In every generation, white society asked itself what to do with the American Indians. Their answers have resulted in the twists and turns of federal Indian policy.

There were two general approaches. One way was to raise the Indians to a "higher level" by "civilizing" them. Zealous missionaries considered it their Christian duty to elevate the Indian through conversion and scanty education. The other approach was to ignore the Indians until they disappeared under pressure from the ever-expanding white society. The myth of the "vanishing Indian" gave stronger support to the latter option, helping to justify the taking of the Indians' land.

Prior to the end of the 18th century, there was no national policy on Indians simply because the American nation had not yet come into existence. American Indians similarly did not possess a political or social unity with which to confront the various Europeans. They were not homogeneous. Rather, they were loosely formed bands and tribes, speaking nearly 300 languages and thousands of dialects. The collective identity felt by Indians today is a result of their common experiences of defeat and/or mistreatment at the hands of whites.

During the colonial period, the British crown did not have a coordinated policy toward the Indians of North America. Specific tribes (most notably the Iroquois and the Cherokee) became military and political pawns used by both the crown and the individual colonies. The success of the American Revolution brought no immediate change. When the United States acquired new territory from France and Mexico in the early 19th century, the federal government wanted to open this land to settlement by homesteaders. But the Indian tribes that lived on this land had signed treaties with European governments assuring their title to the land. Now the United States assumed legal responsibility for honoring these treaties.

At first, President Thomas Jefferson believed that the Louisiana Purchase contained sufficient land for both the Indians and the white population. Within a generation, though, it became clear that the Indians would not be allowed to remain. In the 1830s the federal government began to coerce the eastern tribes to sign treaties agreeing to relinquish their ancestral land and move west of the Mississippi River. Whenever these negotiations failed, President Andrew Jackson used the military to remove the Indians. The southeastern tribes, promised food and transportation during their removal to the West, were instead forced to walk the "Trail of Tears." More than 4,000 men, woman, and children died during this forced march. The "removal policy" was successful in opening the land to homesteaders, but it created enormous hardships for the Indians.

By 1871 most of the tribes in the United States had signed treaties ceding most or all of their ancestral land in exchange for reservations and welfare. The treaty terms were intended to bind both parties for all time. But in the General Allotment Act of 1887, the federal government changed its policy again. Now the goal was to make tribal members into individual landowners and farmers, encouraging their absorption into white society. This policy was advantageous to whites who were eager to acquire Indian land, but it proved disastrous for the Indians. One hundred thirty-eight million acres of reservation land were subdivided into tracts of 160, 80, or as little as 40 acres, and allotted tribe members on an individual basis. Land owned in this way was said to have "trust status" and could not be sold. But the surplus land—all Indian land not allotted to individuals—was opened (for sale) to white settlers. Ultimately, more than 90 million acres of land were taken from the Indians by legal and illegal means.

The resulting loss of land was a catastrophe for the Indians. It was necessary to make it illegal for Indians to sell their land to non-Indians. The Indian Reorganization Act of 1934 officially ended the allotment period. Tribes that voted to accept the provisions of this act were reorganized, and an effort was made to purchase land within preexisting reservations to restore an adequate land base.

Ten years later, in 1944, federal Indian policy again shifted. Now the federal government wanted to get out of the "Indian business." In 1953 an act of Congress named specific tribes whose trust status was to be ended "at the earliest possible time." This new law enabled the United States to end unilaterally, whether the Indians wished it or not, the special status that protected the land in Indian tribal reservations. In the 1950s federal Indian policy was to transfer federal responsibility and jurisdiction to state governments, encourage the physical relocation of Indian peoples from reservations to urban areas, and hasten the termination, or extinction, of tribes.

Between 1954 and 1962 Congress passed specific laws authorizing the termination of more than 100 tribal groups. The stated purpose of the termination policy was to ensure the full and complete integration of Indians into American society. However, there is a less benign way to interpret this legislation. Even as termination was being discussed in Congress, 133 separate bills were introduced to permit the transfer of trust land ownership from Indians to non-Indians.

With the Johnson administration in the 1960s the federal government began to reject termination. In the 1970s yet another Indian policy emerged. Known as "self-determination," it favored keeping the protective role of the federal government while increasing tribal participation in, and control of, important areas of local government. In 1983 President Reagan, in a policy statement on Indian affairs, restated the unique "government is government" relationship of the United States with the Indians. However, federal programs since then have moved toward transferring Indian affairs to individual states, which have long desired to gain control of Indian land and resources.

As long as American Indians retain power, land, and resources that are coveted by the states and the federal government, there will continue to be a "clash of cultures," and the issues will be contested in the courts, Congress, the White House, and even in the international human rights community. To give all Americans a greater comprehension of the issues and conflicts involving American Indians today is a major goal of this series. These issues are not easily understood, nor can these conflicts be readily resolved. The study of North American Indian history and culture is a necessary and important step toward that comprehension. All Americans must learn the history of the relations between the Indians and the federal government, recognize the unique legal status of the Indians, and understand the heritage and cultures of the Indians of North America.

A guard watches at the entrance to the Antelope kiva in the Hopi village of Walpi. Inside the kiva, the sipapu, a hole dug in the ground, symbolizes the place where the Hopi believe their ancestors emerged from underground.

1

THE
EMERGENCE

Long ago, say the Hopi, the earth was covered with water. There was no dry ground. No animals roamed the mountains and plains, no birds flew in the air, and no people lived. But inside the darkened earth dwelled deities and spirits with great knowledge and power.

One day, the goddess of the east and the goddess of the west decided to create living things. They fashioned a bird out of clay and breathed life into it. The bird flew all over the earth and could find no other living creatures. So the goddesses took more clay and made human beings. They gave the people breath and language and sent them on their way.

At that time, the people dwelled inside the earth. At first, their lives were happy and peaceful. They planted their crops and went about their daily tasks. Then it happened that discord arose among the people. They gossiped about each other and argued about many things. Adding to the people's troubles, the rains diminished and the crops ceased to grow. The wisest leaders of

the people knew that they must find a way out. Perhaps they could discover a hole in the surface of the ground so that they could escape from the turmoil below.

Soon afterward, one of the chiefs found a ladder made of reeds, which led up to a hole in the earth. He and the other chiefs led their relatives up the ladder and onto the surface. Each chief carried with him a sacred ear of corn that he intended to plant wherever he and his kin would settle.

The people were glad to emerge from the earth, but they did not know where to make their homes. The chiefs decided to go in separate directions, each accompanied by his followers. They traveled in the four cardinal directions, going north, west, south, and east. After a long time searching, they each found a good place to stay. Happy in their new homeland, the Hopi constructed villages and began to plant crops. And of greatest importance, they pledged to forever recite the prayers and perform the rituals that the powerful deities had given to them when they emerged from the earth.

This story of creation, told by the Hopi since time immemorial, sets out their fundamental principles of life and order in the world. It also gives the people an understanding of the eternal meaning of their beliefs and rituals.

The name *Hopi* means "good in every respect" or "good, peaceable, wise, and knowing." The word captures the essence of the people's desire for wisdom, goodness, and peace. The Hopi have attempted to establish a way of living that puts these great principles into practice. Above all, they desire harmony, balance, and order in their relationships with the world and with other people, creatures, and the forces—such as, according to Hopi belief, gods, goddesses, and spirits—that share the earth with them.

The Hopi strive to live with their families and neighbors according to these ideals of peace and cooperation. They believe that people should help one another, be generous and kind to those in need, and be friendly and good-natured to all.

The Hopi believe that harmony with the natural world comes from knowing one's place in the order of the universe, from knowing that one is a part of the world. People have no right to harm the earth or the creatures living on it but instead should show respect for all of nature's beings.

The physical universe of the Hopi is bounded by four horizontal directions, north, south, east, and west; and by two additional directions, up and down. The points of the four cardinal directions are determined by the four farthest points on the horizon marked by the sun as it rises and sets throughout its yearly cycle of summer and winter solstices. (Actually, from a non-Hopi point of view, these directions would be more accurately described as northwest, southwest, southeast, and northeast.) From their present-day home in the Southwest, the Hopi consider the territory marked off by these points on the horizon to be their ancestral homeland, found centuries ago by the first human beings.

Each direction is associated with a specific color: north is yellow, west is blue, south is red, and east is white. The zenith (upward) is black and the nadir (downward) is speckled with all colors. Links between directions and colors are especially important in the performance of ceremonies. Designs woven into clothing or painted on ritual objects are colored to signify the directions. Through this use of color to symbolize directions, the Hopi re-create the balance and order of the universe.

Each of the six directions is also associated with a specific animal and bird that can be used together in rituals to represent order in the world. The pairings are:

North: mountain lion; oriole
West: bear; bluebird
South: wildcat; parrot
East: wolf; magpie
Zenith: (no animal); tanager
Nadir: mole; (no bird)

A Hopi snake priest photographed near the turn of the century.

In addition to maintaining balance with other people and with the physical world, the Hopi strive for harmony with the world of spirits and mythic beings. To show their respect for spirits, the people recite prayers, make offerings, and perform ceremonies dedicated to deities and the forces of nature. When the Hopi perform their rituals, they believe they are reenacting the deeds of the first humans, who were instructed by the gods. Hopi religious practices therefore link them both to the spirits and to their own ancestors.

In the Hopi view, prayers and rituals are based on principles of reciprocity. People recite prayers to spirits, giving them thanks for their blessing and support. Spirits return the honor by giving the Hopi the aid they requested.

The Hopi think of life and time as continually transforming. Things that appear to be opposites are just different aspects of a continuous, alternating reality. Hopi beliefs about life and death are good examples of this philosophy. When a person dies, the Hopi believe that she or he is born into another world, the world of spirits. At the conclusion of funerals, the Hopi symbolically separate the realms of life and death by drawing four lines of charcoal on the ground as the deceased's body is carried out of the village for burial. A prayer is recited, telling the spirit of the deceased not to harm the living but instead to give blessings just as the living honor the dead.

When a Hopi man or woman dies, a mask made of white cotton is placed over the face. It is called a white cloud mask and symbolizes the clouds that bring rain to Hopi lands. The Hopi believe that the souls of the dead are gradually transformed into clouds and mist. The souls become a liquid essence that is manifested as rain. People pray to the dead, their ancestors, to bless them with the rain that nourishes their crops and ensures their survival.

Beliefs about death thus reveal several themes basic to the Hopi's religion. Life and death are in a continual process of change and transformation. The Hopi believe that reciprocal relations exist between the living and the dead. Through prayers, people honor their ancestors, and through the gift of rain, ancestors make it possible for the living to survive. It is a deeply poetic image of the continuity of bonds created between people and eternally maintained.

Religious practices are central to the Hopi's daily and yearly activities. Indeed, religion is the bedrock of Hopi culture.

Religious ceremonies are held in a special building, called a *kiva* (KEY-va). A kiva is a rectangular structure built completely or partially underground. In either case, it is entered from a trapdoor in the top. A ladder inside the kiva, symbolic of the ladder the first human beings used to emerge onto the earth's surface, descends to the floor, which is divided into two sections. An elevated area provides a place for the public to assemble and observe the ceremonies conducted by ritual practitioners in the lower floor area. On the lower level, a round hole in the ground represents the place where the Hopi ancestors emerged at the time of creation. In other words, kivas symbolize the earth and are a potent reminder to the Hopi of their origins.

In addition to the main room in the kiva where rituals are performed, kivas usually contain a small room where people store ritual gear such as costumes, masks, and musical instruments used during ceremonies.

Hopi rituals usually last eight days, divided into two sets of four. There is also a preliminary day for participants to prepare their costumes and ceremonial objects and to rehearse their songs and dances. During the first four days of each ceremony, secret rites take place inside the kiva. These events are attended only by the villagers actively involved in the ceremony. The participants smoke tobacco pipes, producing clouds of smoke that represent the rain clouds so greatly desired. Worshipers also make offerings and recite prayers to deities.

Ritual participants erect altars in the kiva consisting of vertical wooden or stone slabs that are painted with designs symbolizing corn, lightning, clouds, and various mythic figures. Ceremonial objects are placed before the altar. Among these is a medicine bowl containing fresh spring water. It is set on the ground in the middle of a painting made from colored grains of sand. The sand painting depicts spirit beings whose aid is requested by the people. Around the painting, six lines of different-colored cornmeal are drawn to represent the six directions. Altars and ceremonial objects remain in place dur-

A section of a painted mural found by archaeologists on a kiva wall in the Hopi village of Awatovi. On the right is a warrior holding a bow and arrows; on the left is a squash-woman. The murals were painted as part of religious ceremonies and were later painted over so as not to be seen by unauthorized persons.

ing the entire period when the ritual is being performed, but on the next to last day, the altar is dismantled, the sand painting is erased, and the ritual objects are put away for safekeeping.

The second set of four days, or second half of each ceremony, is devoted to public dances and festivities. Some of

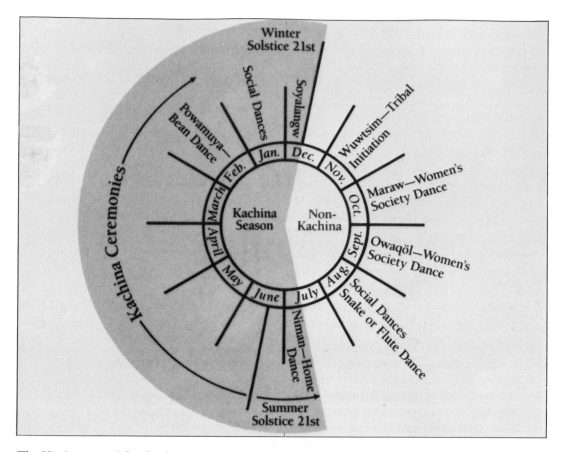

The Hopi ceremonial calendar: Although important ceremonies are conducted in each month of the year, kachinas visit the Hopi towns only during the six months between the winter and summer solstices. During the rest of the year they are believed to return to their homes on the San Francisco Peaks.

these activities take place in the kiva and may be attended by adult members of the community. Others occur in open plazas in the village and are viewed by all. Public rituals are lively events. Everyone enjoys listening to the beautiful music and songs and watching the skilled dancers. It is also a time of feasting, socializing, and renewing of friendship and community bonds.

Throughout all the days devoted to a ceremony, ritual participants must observe a number of taboos, or restrictions, on their behavior. They must abstain from sexual activity, and they are not permitted to eat any salt or meat. At night, they sleep in the kiva, away from the distractions of everyday life. These restrictions are also in force for four days after the ritual.

On the last day of a ceremony, participants conduct a rite of purification, sprinkling ashes on themselves and on the special objects used in the ceremony. The Hopi believe that the spiritual powers that have come to them during the religious ceremonies are dangerous if they are treated casually. Therefore, when ritual practitioners return to normal life, they must purify themselves to avoid getting sick from the strength of the powers with which they have come in contact.

Hopi ceremonies occur at fixed times throughout the year. The ritual calendar is divided into two equal periods. One begins in late January or early February and lasts until the middle of July. The other occupies the remaining months until the cycle is renewed in the following year. Each period contains a different set of ceremonies. Ritual leaders choose specific dates for most rituals by observing the sun's position as it rises over particular landmarks on the horizon. Some rites are timed in accordance with the phases of the moon.

During the time from February through July, most of the rituals concern a group of spirit beings called *kachinas* (ka-CHEE-na). Kachinas are the spirits of ancestors. They are believed to live in mountains on the borders of Hopi territory. The Hopi recite prayers and give offerings to the kachinas so that they will aid their human descendants, especially by bringing the rain so vital to their crops.

On certain religious occasions, Hopi men impersonate kachina spirits and appear in Hopi villages, where they are honored at ceremonies. When kachinas visit the people, they are dressed in colorful costumes and jewelry. Their heads are covered with beautiful masks and large headdresses adorned with feathers. Some kachinas take the form of animals or birds, such as the owl, the eagle, and the bear. Others are named after a distinctive feature of their appearance, such as the Long-Bearded or the Left-Handed. While they visit the Hopi, kachinas give presents of food and other items to the villagers, who respond with thanks and prayers.

Kachinas enter villages at sunrise. They proceed in a line led by their ritual father. The kachinas follow a path made of cornmeal, advancing with dance steps to the kivas where they will be honored by the villagers. Ritual leaders await the kachinas in the kiva and conduct ceremonies dedicated to these ancestral spirits. Other adults may enter the kiva and observe the rites. Children who have been initiated into the kiva may also attend.

During the period of kachina rituals, initiations are conducted for girls and boys to make them members of the kiva society. Children are initiated when they are between six and nine years old. The rites are held each spring for groups of children who have reached the appropriate age. Parents begin by choosing a ceremonial mother or ceremonial father for their daughter or son. Sponsors prepare the children for membership in a kiva by teaching them about their duties as a participant in the society. Later, at

A young Hopi girl holds the gifts brought by the kachinas in a 1989 ceremony. When the kachinas leave the villages, they often give small images of themselves as presents to Hopi children. The dolls are not toys to be played with, but images to help the children learn about the kachinas.

the appointed time, the sponsor leads the child to the kiva for initiation.

The initiation rite, called *kachinvaki*, consists of prayers and songs that teach children about the spirit world. In addition, boys and girls are encouraged to behave properly, to treat other people with kindness, and to respect and honor the spirits. Then the masked kachinas make their appearance in the kiva. One of the kachinas carries branches of yucca, a plant that grows wild in the desert. Another kachina takes a yucca branch and whips each of the children in turn. The young children are frightened to be in the presence of these powerful spirits. But at the end of the ritual, when the kachina figures take off their masks, the children see that the kachinas standing before them are their relatives and neighbors.

Ritual leaders explain to the children that even though living men impersonate kachina spirits, the kachinas themselves watch and approve the proceedings. The powerful essence of the real kachinas comes to the Hopi even though it is embodied by human beings. This is perhaps the most important religious lesson revealed to children at their initiation. They learn that spiritual power affects humans even though it cannot be seen.

The last major ritual of the kachina cycle is called *Niman*. It occurs in mid-July. Niman signals the departure of the kachinas, who leave the Hopi to return to their spirit world. Niman is a festive dance at which people bid farewell to kachinas for the year. The kachinas reciprocate the people's good wishes by distributing toys to all the children. Girls receive wooden dolls dressed in kachina costumes and masks. Boys are given bows and arrows.

Before the kachinas depart from the villages, a special prayer is recited to them:

> When you return to your homes bring this message to them that, without delay, they may have mercy for us with their liquid essence [rain] so that all things will grow and life may be bountiful.

This prayer reaffirms, once again, the eternal bond between the kachinas, the ancestral spirits, and their human descendants. The Hopi believe that just as they need the kachinas, the kachinas need the Hopi. This is in part the basis for the belief that if the Hopi fulfill their responsibilities toward the kachinas, then the kachinas will fulfill their responsibilities toward the Hopi by sending rain.

After the period of kachina rituals ends in July, a new cycle of religious ceremonies begins. Several different festivals take place, each of which is organized and conducted by members of various ritual societies. People become members of these societies by going through a rite of initiation. During initiations, people learn their duties as members of the society. They are taught the prayers, songs, and dances that they will perform at the ceremonies.

The first ritual performed is the Snake and Antelope festival. Snake and Antelope ceremonies occur in alternate years. They each consist of dances and races conducted by members of the Snake and Antelope societies. The Flute Society performs its own ritual dances in late summertime.

Kachina dolls are made from the dried roots of cottonwood trees. Every detail of the kachinas' costumes has symbolic meaning. The color on a doll's mask, for example, indicates the direction from which a kachina comes. In the Hopi world view, there are six cardinal directions.

In autumn, women's ritual societies conduct three separate ceremonies called *Maraw, Lakan,* and *Owaqol.* They are primarily concerned with ensuring women's fertility and the fertility of corn, the earth, and all the plants.

Next come the rituals of the four men's societies. Their names are *Wuwuchim, Agave,* Horn, and Singers. Wuwuchim is the most important of the men's rituals. It includes an elaborate initiation rite, beginning with a ceremonial lighting of a new fire to symbolize a boy's new birth into the society. After Wuwuchim, the other men's rituals are performed. Agave is dedicated to success in war; the Horn Dance is directed at ensuring a good hunting season; and the Singers ritual is concerned with human fertility.

Finally, the last ritual of the yearly cycle occurs each December at the time of the winter solstice. It is called *Soyal*, and its purpose is to renew the earth and the life-giving forces upon which the Hopi depend. During Soyal, painted wooden sticks, called prayer sticks, are buried in the ground. They contain prayers that the Hopi believe help maintain the universe and ensure the earth's bounty.

In addition to the society members who organize and participate in specific ceremonies, ritual clowns play a very important role in the public part of many religious festivals. Clowns are men who dress in brightly colored costumes and paint their bodies and faces with intricate designs. Clowns entertain observers with their comic imitations of animals, birds, and people. They may speak in riddles, shout obscenities, or tease bystanders.

But Hopi clowns also mete out discipline and warnings to people in the community who have behaved inappropriately, injuring their neighbors. Perhaps someone in the village is known to be uncooperative, lazy, or argumentative. Such an individual may be singled out by a clown during a public ritual. The clown then loudly ridicules and insults the wrongdoer in the presence of all onlookers. He may spill a pail of water on his target or even whip the offender with tree branches. This public confrontation usually makes targets feel ashamed and leads them to change their behavior.

Finally, clowns serve the purpose of teaching people about the limits of acceptable human behavior by giving a negative example. Clowns do outrageous things not permitted to ordinary people. They may use obscene language, imitate sexual acts, and even urinate or defecate in public. Such actions are, of course, intolerable in normal society. But by shocking people with their behavior, clowns teach the rules of proper social living. Their behavior is tolerated because they are considered to be deities and thus sacred. The Hopi also understand that they are reversing normal behavior: this is why they are clowns. Although the Hopi villagers may be surprised and entertained by the clowns' antics, they also are reminded of cultural norms of etiquette shared by members of the community.

Hopi attitudes toward religion include both actions and thoughts. The Hopi believe that conducting rituals, performing sacred dances and songs, and reciting prayers helps establish harmony and balance in the universe. Through these activities, the Hopi show respect to deities and spirit beings. And in return, spirits bestow blessings and bounty on the people. But in addition to performing the proper actions, people must have a "good heart." To the Hopi this means controlling one's emotions, being kind to others, and keeping one's thoughts focused on peace and on harmony. ▲

Anasazi ruins at Canyon de Chelly, Arizona. The Anasazi are the probable ancestors of the Hopi. They built their homes in high places with very limited access as a means of protection from their enemies, a tactic that the Hopi later emulated when they moved their villages to the tops of mesas to protect themselves from the Spanish.

ORIGINS

The Southwest region of the United States has been inhabited by Native Americans for at least 10,000 years. Over many millennia, these peoples developed cultures that relied on nearby natural resources for food and equipment. The Hopi are one of numerous Indian groups descended from the original inhabitants of the Southwest. Hopi culture shares many characteristic features with other peoples known collectively by Europeans and Americans as the Pueblo Indians. They are called this because the Spanish word *pueblo* means "town." It is the word the Spaniards used for the Hopi and similar Indian tribes that lived in permanent villages of multistoried adobe dwellings.

The Southwest is majestic, endowed with mountains, desert lands, plateaus, mesas, and deep canyons. It rises high above sea level to altitudes of 5,000 to 7,000 feet. The climate is arid, with rainfall averaging only between 10 and 15 inches per year. There are also relatively few permanently flowing rivers in the Southwest. The lack of both rain and flowing water makes survival in the region extremely difficult. Despite the harshness of the environment, many forms of plant and animal life have been able to adapt to it. The desert contains many varieties of natural vegetation, including roots, grasses, plants, and cacti. Juniper and piñon trees are also scattered throughout the area. Small animals, especially rabbits, desert rodents, and reptiles, are quite numerous. In the mountains dotted throughout the Southwest, larger animals such as deer, antelope, bear, and foxes can be found.

Native Americans were able to adapt to the desert by using their ingenuity. Indigenous peoples utilized the varied plant and animal life that had adapted to the desert for their food. They also made use of plants, roots, stone, and wood to craft household utensils and tools.

Researchers today divide the prehistoric epoch of the southwestern Indians into several distinct periods, each of which is marked by specific cultural developments. Major eras in the Southwest include the Desert Tradition, which began approximately 10,000 years ago and lasted until 300 B.C.; the Mogollon Tradition, which endured from 300 B.C. to A.D. 1100; and the Anasazi Tradition, which began in A.D. 1100 and ended in the 16th century.

The culture of the earliest peoples in the Southwest is called the Desert Tradition. Sites inhabited by Desert people have been discovered at Concho in present-day eastern Arizona and at Bat Cave and Tularosa Cave in northern and central New Mexico.

Desert people depended on wild plants and animals for their food supply. In addition to the flora and fauna familiar to us today, several species of large animals roamed throughout the region thousands of years ago. Some of these animals, such as horses, elephants, and great bison, have become extinct in North America but were numerous in prehistoric times. They were hunted by native peoples to provide food as well as hides used for clothing and shelter.

In addition to hunting large and small animals, Desert people created a technology for preparing and cooking

Several Hopi villages are situated atop Second Mesa. Shipaulovi is on top of the mesa on the rocky hill on the left; Mishongnovi is on the smaller hill in the center.

plant foods. They had many kinds of grinding stones, called *metates*, for grinding seeds and nuts.

Because they depended on natural resources for their survival, Desert people did not have permanent settlements. Instead, they shifted their camps from time to time in order to gather wild plants and to hunt migrating animals. Camps were fairly small, consisting of no more than a few families. Populations had to be limited due to the scarcity of permanent sources of food.

Desert people continued their foraging way of life for many thousands of years. Then, approximately 5,000 years ago, they learned how to grow some of their own food. Corncobs have been discovered in prehistoric Desert sites dating from that time. Presumably, Desert people learned the art of agriculture from native peoples in Mexico. Farming technology gradually spread from central Mexico northward into the Southwest through a process called cultural diffusion, the borrowing of skills by one group from a neighboring group.

For 2,000 years after the beginnings of farming in Desert societies, corn was the only crop grown. Then, about 3,000 years ago, native peoples added new crops, especially varieties of beans and squash. Corn, beans, and squash have since remained the staple foods of southwestern peoples, including the modern Pueblo Indians.

Despite the incorporation of farming into their economies, Desert people did not abandon their previous way of life. They still lived in small groups and did

not settle permanently in a fixed location. They also continued to hunt animals in the desert and mountains and to gather wild plants, nuts, and roots.

In 300 B.C., a profound change in native culture took place. A new culture, or tradition, called Mogollon, developed. Mogollon people constructed permanent villages. They built rectangular or circular houses made of clay and stone. The Mogollon clustered houses together in small settlements so that approximately one hundred people lived in a typical Mogollon village, such as those found at Forestdale and Black River in Arizona and at Cibola and Mimbres in New Mexico.

Mogollon people also added several very important innovations to the existing stock of equipment. Perhaps of greatest significance, they began to make earthen pottery. Pots, bowls, and jars of various sizes and shapes were used for cooking, carrying, and storing foods and other supplies. Mogollon people fashioned many types of grinding stones, mortars, and pestles for preparing plant foods. They also began to use bows and arrows for hunting. Tools, utensils, and weapons were made from stone, bone, wood, and shell.

The next period of cultural change began about A.D. 1100. This new tradition is called the Anasazi. Anasazi people inhabited a large area, covering present-day New Mexico, most of Arizona, and the southern portions of Utah and Colorado. The largest Anasazi villages were concentrated in the region known today as the Four Corners, the

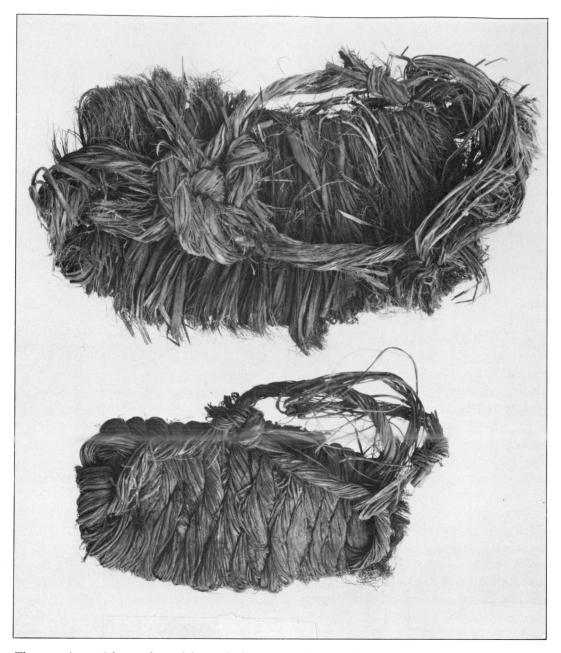

These ancient wickerwork sandals, made from yucca leaves, are believed to have been worn by the Mogollon people, ancestors of the Hopi. They were found when Tularosa Cave in New Mexico was excavated.

area around the point where the borders of Arizona, New Mexico, Utah, and Colorado meet. Typical Anasazi settlements include Canyon de Chelly and Kayenta in Arizona, Mesa Verde in Colorado, and Chaco Canyon in New Mexico.

Anasazi villages consisted of numerous rectangular houses, built of one, two, or three stories. Houses were adjacent to each other, forming rows of dwellings lined along streets. Towns also had open courtyards or plazas amidst the houses. Anasazi villages were much larger than settlements in previous periods, having populations of one thousand or more. Some of the largest sites, such as Point of Pines in northern Arizona, were inhabited by between 2,000 and 3,000 people in the 14th century.

The Anasazi utilized two different sources of water for their farmlands. They made use of floodwater by planting their crops near streams that overflowed during heavy rainstorms, and they diverted water from streams, channeling it into their fields.

Sometime in the 14th century, large Anasazi villages were suddenly abandoned. Most researchers today suggest that drastic climatic changes account for the movement of people to other locations and for the decrease in the size of towns. As the climate became more arid, sources of water diminished. Native peoples were forced to leave their villages to resettle in other areas. From that time on, different groups of Indians in the Southwest became culturally distinct. They are each identified by their

This ladle made of pottery was crafted by the Anasazi.

own names, such as the Hopi, Zuni, Tewa, Keres, and Towa. Some groups moved along the Rio Grande in what is now New Mexico and established villages there. They used the river's waters to irrigate their farms. Other people, including the Hopi, remained in desert lands in present-day northeastern Arizona. Although these people stayed in their traditional territory, they shifted the location of some of their settlements in order to adjust the population size to the available resources.

By the middle of the 14th century, these Hopi settlements underwent some dramatic changes. Until that time, the

Hopi had lived either in small villages or isolated farmsteads. They were concentrated in northern Arizona, near Kayenta and Black Mesa. But during the 100 years from about 1350 to 1450, the Hopi abandoned Kayenta because of climatic changes and drought. Hopi villages farther south grew rapidly in size as more Hopi relocated there. Hopi villages were located at or near their present-day sites south of Black Mesa in an area approximately 60 miles wide. Villages were typically inhabited by between 500 and 1,000 people.

The location of Hopi settlements was advantageous for farming. Since they were situated south of Black Mesa, strong winds blew sand from the mesa onto Hopi territory, forming sand dunes that retained moisture. The Hopi then planted their crops near the dunes, benefiting from the moisture in the soil. They built windbreaks of brush and stone to keep the high winds from damaging their crops.

Over the centuries, the Hopi had skillfully developed strains of corn and beans that were adapted to dry conditions. The plants had very long roots, sometimes 15 or 20 feet in length. These roots secured the plants in the ground and enabled them to withstand strong gusts of wind. Long roots also made it possible for plants to absorb whatever moisture was in the soil.

In the 14th century, the Hopi invented a new style of pottery. Although all Pueblo peoples made pottery, Hopi decorative styles changed considerably. In previous centuries, pottery was painted with black-on-white geometric designs. But Hopi women began to use black-on-orange, black-on-yellow, and multicolor decorations. Their innovative designs testify to an explosion of artistic imagination and skill. In addition to the geometric forms, they painted sweeping curved lines and naturalistic figures. Subject matter included various animals, birds, flowers, and human beings. Both individual figures and group scenes were depicted.

Hopi artists also painted dramatic murals on walls of buildings that they used for conducting ceremonies. The multicolor paintings showed scenes of animals, humans, and mythological figures. They were used during rituals to represent characters and events in myths. After a ceremony ended, the murals were washed over with a coating of plain plaster. When the Hopi performed another ceremony, a new mural was painted on the wall. Modern researchers at a Hopi settlement called Awatovi have recently found walls with 100 layers of plaster. Of these, 30 layers contained paintings.

Coal mining was another cultural development unique to the Hopi. In the 14th century, they began to mine coal found near their villages. Hopis most often used the technique of strip-mining. They removed surface soil and dug out the coal situated underneath. Their tools included picks, scrapers, and hammerstones. The Hopi extracted coal that lay deeper beneath the surface by constructing underground mines. Researchers today estimate that some Hopi

Corn discovered in archaeological digs indicates that the Hopis' ancestors selectively bred the vegetable so that the ears became longer and bore larger kernels. The corn on the top row is the oldest; that on the bottom row is from more recent times.

This black-on-red jar used for storing seeds was excavated at Oraibi, a present-day Hopi settlement that is the longest continually occupied place in the United States. The jar dates from approximately 1,000 years ago. The Hopi were the first Pueblo tribe to use colors other than black and white on their pottery.

communities in the 14th through 16th centuries extracted as much as 450 pounds of coal each day. Approximately 30,000 tons were mined by residents of Awatovi during a period that lasted three centuries.

The Hopi employed coal for many purposes, including cooking, heating, firing pottery, and pigmenting ceramics and paintings. They saved the ash from coal fires and used it as a bed for flagstones that formed the floors of their houses. The Hopi also constructed stoves with chimneys, apparently in reaction to the noxious smoke made by burning coal.

In sum, Hopi culture contained many features common to all the Pueblo. They lived in houses and villages built on a Pueblo model and grew crops common throughout the region. But the Hopi also developed unique traits, using their own skills, inventions, and artistic imagination.

Pueblo peoples like the Hopi remained in the Southwest into the historic period, that is, the 16th century. Although the Spanish who arrived in the area in the 16th century referred to all the natives by the same term, the Pueblo had distinct cultures and spoke different languages. They also lived in numerous villages throughout the region. Native peoples who resided in villages along the Rio Grande in New Mexico called themselves by such names as Tewa, Towa, Tano, and Keres. Farther to the west, the Hopi and other indigenous peoples such as the Zuni made their homes.

Languages spoken by the Pueblo are quite diverse. Several completely different language families are represented. The Hopi language belongs to a family called Uto-Aztecan, distantly related to the language spoken by the Aztecs in Mexico. The language of the nearby Zuni is not related to Hopi. Linguists today are uncertain as to whether Zuni is a "language isolate" with no known connections or whether it belongs to a family called Penutian. If Zuni is a Penutian language, it is a remote relative of languages spoken in parts of California. Pueblo living in towns along the Rio Grande speak languages belonging to two other families, called Tanoan and Keresan.

In addition to the Pueblo, other Indian tribes lived in the Southwest. Some of these groups were on friendly terms with the Hopi and traded with them. Such farming peoples as the Pima, Papago, and Havasupai inhabited parts of western Arizona. Contact between them and the Hopi was intermittent but generally peaceful.

Other groups in the region had a very different way of life. The Ute from present-day Utah and the Navajo who lived in what is now Arizona and New Mexico occasionally supplemented their own economies by raiding sedentary Hopi villages. They took crops, turkeys, and other goods from the fields and towns. In these raids, people on both sides were sometimes killed. But despite occasional conflict, the Hopi also traded with the Ute and the Navajo.

Through the centuries, the Hopi considered themselves safe and secure in their ancient homeland. They had a rich cultural history on which to build their future. ▲

A Hopi woman prepares piki, a traditional bread that is a staple of the Hopi diet. Hopi women occupy a prominent place in their culture: women own all Hopi land, and when a man marries, he moves into his wife's house.

THE
HOPI
WORLD

The Hopi live on land that is beautiful and majestic. Yet they also live in an environment that presents enormous problems for people pursuing a way of life dependent on farming. The Southwest region is extremely arid, with few sources of water. There are a small number of permanent springs in the area from which people can get drinking water, but these springs do not supply enough water to irrigate fields. No permanent rivers or streams flow in Hopi territory.

In this context, the Hopi are forced to depend on rain as the only source of water for their farmlands. But rain cannot provide security. Annual rainfall is relatively slight, averaging only 10 inches per year. In some years, there is not enough rain, and then crops dry out and die. In other years, summer rains come in sudden torrential downpours that drown the young and growing plants. The people hope for good years of balanced rainfall, sufficient but not excessive.

The growing season itself is relatively short. Even though spring and summer days are sunny and warm, the high altitude of Hopi land results in sharp differences in temperature between day and night. At altitudes of 6,000 feet, nighttime frosts come early in the fall and harm immature plants.

Because resources are uncertain, villages are relatively small, with most towns having around 500 residents. Populations have to be small in order to keep within the limits of farming in a desert environment.

Hopi villages are permanent, having maintained their locations for at least 700 years. Before the arrival of the Spanish, there were six main town sites and perhaps a few smaller ones dispersed throughout the territory. The major towns were called Walpi (WAL-pi; "place of the ravine"), Awatovi (a-WA-to-bi), Oraibi (o-RAY-bi; "gray-rock place"), Mishongnovi (mi-SHONG-no-vi; "large boulder"), Shongopavi (shong-GO-pa-vi; "sand-grass spring place"), and Shipaulovi (shi-POW-lo-vi; "place of mosquitoes").

All Hopi villages are built on the same plan. They consist of clay and stone houses that are placed next to each other along rows forming streets. Houses contain from one to several square rooms and may be one, two, or three stories high.

Villages also have one or more kivas in which rituals are performed. In addition, each village contains at least one large open courtyard or plaza where people gather and hold public dances and rituals. Houses line the plazas, providing places from which people can view communal events.

Families who live together in a house are related through a system of kinship that anthropologists call a lineage. A lineage is a group of people who claim descent from a common ancestor. Hopi lineages follow lines of descent through women. This is what anthropologists call a matrilineal system, a term meaning "mother's line."

Households typically consist of an elder woman, her husband, their daughters, and their unmarried sons. When a man marries, he goes to live with his wife's family. Married women remain with their own families. A large number of people may reside together in one house, helping each other with family tasks and looking after each other's children.

The senior woman in a household has great influence over other members. She gives advice about family matters and plans and coordinates joint activities. Her eldest daughter also has much influence in the household. She assumes her mother's duties when the elder woman is away from home and will succeed to the position of household leader after the mother's death.

Although men move to their wives' homes, they maintain strong ties to their parents and relatives. A man visits his kin frequently. He takes part in family events and may serve as a disciplinarian to his sisters' children. Hopi men often consider the households of their mothers and sisters to be their real homes.

The senior woman of each lineage sets aside a room in her house for the storage of ceremonial objects. Such items as masks, tobacco pipes, religious figurines, rattles, and feathers are kept there. The most important ritual object safeguarded in the room is a sacred ear of corn symbolizing the lineage and its members. The corn is carefully wrapped in cloth and feathers and kept on an altar especially erected for it.

The Hopi system of kinship also contains units called clans. A clan is a grouping of people who consider themselves to be related although they may not be able to trace their actual relationship to one another. A clan may consist of hundreds of people. It is different from a lineage, which typically contains a smaller number of known relatives in a direct line of descent. Just as Hopi lineages are based on descent through women, membership in clans also follows matrilineal principles. A child automatically belongs to its mother's clan.

The Hopi village of Mishongnovi, with its central plaza and houses of several stories built next to one another, is typical of traditional Hopi towns. People usually live in the upper stories of the pueblos, which they reach both by ladders and stairs; the lower levels of the dwellings are used primarily for storage.

Hopi clans are named after animals, birds, foods, natural substances, and objects. For example, some clans have bird names: Sparrow, Hawk, Parrot, Dove, Eagle, Bluebird; others are named after mammals, reptiles, or insects: Badger, Bear, Coyote, Snake, Lizard, Butterfly; some have the names of foods: Corn, Squash; and others are named for various plants and substances: Sand, Fog, Snow, Reed, Cactus.

One of the older women in each clan is designated as the head of the clan. She is called the clan mother. Clan mothers make decisions regarding members of their clan, help settle disputes among them, and give advice about family matters. When the head of a clan dies, the next oldest woman in the group usually succeeds to her position.

The brother of a clan mother also has a prominent place in clan activities, and his opinions and advice carry much weight. He also plays an important role in organizing and conducting family ceremonies.

Every Hopi belongs to a clan, which is one of the most important features of Hopi social organization. Membership in a clan descends through the mother. The symbols of the major clan mothers of the village of Shongopovi are (left to right, top to bottom): Eagle, Sun's Forehead, Sun, Fog, Snow, Snake, Strap, Spider, Bluebird, Cloud, Bear, Antelope, Parrot-Kachina, Otter, and Corn.

People within each clan follow certain rules of behavior. First of all, they cannot marry members of their own clan. A child's mother and father must therefore be members of different groups. The Hopi also believe that one should not marry a member of one's father's clan. Violating this rule is not as serious as marrying within one's own group but it is considered improper and is rarely done.

Clan members help each other in times of crisis. If someone's crops have failed, or if someone is ill or in distress, clanmates should lend economic or emotional support and comfort. Although the Hopi believe that all people should be kind, generous, and helpful to others, clanmates should be especially so.

In addition to their social functions, clans are landholding units. Hopi land is not owned by individuals but rather by clans. Each clan has its specific territory, marked by boundary stones at the corners. The stones are painted with symbols representing the group. Clan mothers divide clan land among the women who are heads of lineages. These women then assign portions of the land to their daughters and their daughters' families.

Each family is given access to farmland in several locations. Since the Hopi live in a climate where there are extremes of rainfall and temperature, they can never be certain that plants grown in any particular place will succeed. For example, some land may be on higher or lower ground; some may be closer or farther from streams or places where runoffs from summer rains tend to accumulate. Because of this uncertainty, it is essential for Hopi farmers to distribute their crops in a number of locations, hoping that at least some of them will fare well. It is for this same reason that the head of a household gives her daughters sections of farmland in various areas under her control.

Before the arrival of Europeans in North America, the Hopi followed a division of labor based on gender—that is, each gender was assigned different economic tasks. Men were the farmers. They prepared fields, planted and tended crops, and harvested them in the summer and in fall when they ripened. Before a man married, he helped his father farm the land given to his mother. After marriage, a man worked on land under his wife's control.

Hopi farmers grew various crops to support themselves and their families. Several types of corn were the staples of the diet, including white, blue, and sweet corn. Numerous varieties of beans and squash supplemented corn dishes. The planting season began in April when men planted the first crop of corn. This batch was ready for harvest in mid-July, in time for the kachina Niman ceremony. In May, men planted more corn, along with beans and squash. Men also planted tobacco and cotton in former times. They wove cotton into cloth and then fashioned clothing, blankets, and sashes for their families. The harvest period lasted from late summer through autumn, depending on the growing season for each variety of plant.

In addition to farming, men hunted near their villages for small animals such as rabbits and other desert rodents. They occasionally traveled farther into the mountains surrounding Hopi territory to hunt antelope and deer.

Men made the tools they used for farming and hunting. Farm implements were fairly simple, being for the most part digging sticks, wooden shovels, and stone axes. Hunting gear consisted of wooden bows and arrows tipped with stone arrowheads. Men also made the weapons and shields that they used in warfare, and they wove the baskets used for carrying or storing food and equip-ment. Other necessary tasks performed by men included cutting and hauling the firewood used for cooking and for heating houses in the very cold winters. Finally, crafting beautiful jewelry from stones of turquoise, shell, and coral was also a male occupation.

Hopi women were responsible for work within the household. They prepared corn for cooking by first shelling corn kernels and grinding them into a fine meal. Each household owned three grinding stones called metates that were kept in a large wooden frame when not in use. The stones were distinguished by the thickness of their edges so that they

A Hopi Indian throws corn into an underground furnace to roast it. Just as corn holds a central place in the Hopi diet, it also holds great prominence in the Hopi religion, symbolizing life. Hopi children are given their names in a ceremony in which a perfect ear of white corn, tsotsmingwu, is passed over the baby four times.

Hopi women grinding corn on metates early in this century. The hair worn in side whorls indicates that the women have reached puberty but have not married.

produced cornmeal of different degrees of coarseness. They could be used in succession in order to make the finest powder.

Households also owned a cooking stone called a *piki* stone that women used to make piki, one of the Hopi's most prized foods even today. Piki is a wafer-thin bread made of fine blue cornmeal. Women begin by building a fire under the piki stone and spreading cottonseed oil on its surface. Then they spread a thin batter of cornmeal on the hot stone. When the bread is cooked, the woman peels it off and rolls it or folds it for serving. Piki is eaten at daily meals as well as on ceremonial occasions.

Other dishes of corn breads and hominy were regularly eaten. In addition, Hopi women prepared several varieties of beans. When beans were harvested, they were dried and stored for later use. When the Hopi were ready to eat them, they boiled and roasted the dried beans. Meals often included different types of squash. Women boiled or roasted meat when it was available. Some meat was supplied by the efforts of men who hunted the animals, but the Hopi also traditionally kept large flocks of turkeys that they used for food.

Women made pottery, including bowls used for cooking and serving food. They crafted many different kinds of earthen containers used for storing corn and other essential items.

Finally, women had primary responsibility for caring for their children as well as for general household tasks. They periodically plastered the walls in their houses with fresh layers of mud in order to keep the walls unbroken and the rooms clean.

Relationships between Hopi women and men were based on their philosophy of balance and reciprocity. Men and women learned different skills and performed different tasks, but they were considered equally important and valuable. Men depended on women for the work they did, and women depended on men's labor as well; each contributed to their family's survival.

The Hopi made extensive use of many varieties of plants growing naturally in the environment. Some of these were eaten, some were used as medicines, and others had household or personal purposes. For example, roots of the yucca plant produce a soapy substance that is used for hair washing. Hair washing was not only part of personal hygiene but was also an important feature of many rituals, including ceremonies marking the naming of babies, girls' puberty rites, and marriages.

In traditional times, men wore woven cotton shirts and aprons over deerskin leggings. Women wore woven blouses and skirts. Clothing was sometimes brightly embroidered with contrasting colors and designs. Both women and men adorned themselves with sashes, necklaces, and other articles of turquoise and shell jewelry. To protect their feet, they wore moccasins and boots made of deer or antelope hide.

Scenes of life in Hopi villages can be summed up by the words of Antonio de Espejo, leader of a Spanish expedition through Pueblo territory in 1582:

As we crossed this province the inhabitants of each town came out to meet us, took us to their pueblos, and gave us quantities of turkeys, corn, beans, and tortillas, with other kinds of bread which they make skillfully. . . . They grind raw corn on very large stones, five or six women working together, and from the flour they make many kinds of bread. Their houses are two, three, or four stories high, each house being partitioned into a number of rooms. In this province, some of the natives are clad in cotton blankets or dressed deer skins. The women have cotton skirts, often embroidered with colored thread, and over their shoulders a blanket fastened at the waist by a strip of embroidered material, with tassels. The women arrange their hair neatly and prettily.

Young Hopi women fashioned their hair into a distinctive style when they reached puberty. They parted their hair in the middle and formed each half into a tight pinwheel on either side of their head above the ear. Young women adopted this hairstyle after puberty but abandoned it when they married.

Hopi marriages were marked by ceremonial exchanges of gifts between a prospective bride and groom. Before her wedding, a bride-to-be spent four days in her mother-in-law's household grinding cornmeal and making piki bread. This bread became the feast meal served at the wedding. During the same period, male relatives of the groom went to a kiva where they spun cotton into cloth and made wedding clothes for the bride. The men were later thanked by the bride and her female relatives with gifts of piki.

The exchange of gifts at marriages symbolically expressed the balance and reciprocity of women's and men's work.

By giving piki bread to their mothers-in-law, brides offered food typically produced by women. And by giving clothing to the bride, male relatives of the groom offered products normally made by men.

Throughout Hopi history, family life has emphasized the ideals of harmony and cooperation among members. People are expected to help one another, to be generous in sharing what they have, and to treat each other with kindness and respect. The Hopi like people who are even-tempered and refrain from showing anger or engaging in arguments.

Children are taught these values by the example and words of their elders. A young child is showered with affection and attention. The child is liberally indulged by all adults during its first two years of life. But when a child reaches the age of two, an age distinguished by the ability to walk, parental attitudes change. The child is then considered to be responsible for his or her actions. Adults teach children norms of proper behavior and the values of Hopi life. Children are also trained to endure discomforts or displeasure without complaining.

Children who misbehave are admonished by their parents and other family members. They may be sternly lectured by their mother's brother when he returns home for visits. In addition, adults may threaten children by telling them that ogres or giants will come and whip them or carry them away. Indeed,

A woman from Oraibi pueblo holds the reed container for her wedding clothes, which were woven for her by male relatives of the groom. Just as pottery was traditionally made only by Hopi women, weaving was a traditional male activity.

from time to time, two men dressed in special clothing and frightening masks walk through the village and act as disciplinarians. When parents see these men approach their house, they tell their children to hide so that they will not be caught. But if a child misbehaves often, its parents may arrange in advance for the disciplinarians to come to the house, find the child, and give the girl or boy a forceful scolding or a light whipping.

Since Hopi villages are relatively small, it is not necessary to have an extensive set of political officials to govern the town. Each village, though, has a town chief, called *kikmongwi* (kik-MON-wee), a title meaning "leader of the house." While a kikmongwi gives advice and has influence over others, these chiefs have no absolute power to enforce decisions. It is not surprising that in a society in which everything is understood within a religious context the kikmongwi's most important functions are ritual; that they supervise the planning and preparation of village ceremonies is considered much more important than any political role they play.

Town chiefs are selected by a village council made up of leaders of all the clans represented in the village. Clan leaders also serve as advisors and assistants to the town chief. A town chief must be a man belonging to the Bear clan. Other qualifications are personal characteristics. He should be intelligent, even-tempered, kind, and generous to others. He should be a good farmer and a reliable and cooperative member of his

family and community. In the words of Leslie White, an anthropologist and observer of Hopi life, a town chief behaves as follows:

> The chief should hold himself somewhat aloof from the daily and mundane affairs of the [village]; he is supposed to concentrate on spiritual affairs. He should take no part in any quarrels. Everyone should treat him with kindness and respect. And the chief should have only kindly feelings toward his people.

A town chief holds his position for life. However, if he becomes arrogant or abuses his rights, or if he shows himself to be incompetent, he can be removed from office by the village council of clan leaders.

Each town chief has a special assistant called a town crier. This man has the duty of making public announcements on behalf of the chief or at the request of heads of the various ritual associations. The crier climbs to the rooftop of one of the central houses in the village and makes his announcement for all to hear. Messages usually relate to the timing of such events as the beginning of the planting season or upcoming community ceremonies.

Each Hopi village is considered a separate political entity. There is no formal structure uniting the towns into any sort of larger unit. Decisions are made within each village and affect only residents of that town.

The Hopi have no system of formal laws dictating how people should behave or setting punishments for wrongdoers. But an individual's actions come under the collective scrutiny of family and neighbors. People who wrong others may be reprimanded by the head of their household or lineage. They may become targets of gossip and be teased about their actions by anyone in the community. When people meet with such public criticism, they usually correct their behavior and try to avoid any further slights to others.

The Hopi believe that people who commit wrongful acts or think bad thoughts may become ill. In keeping with their philosophy of harmony and balance, the Hopi think that disease can come from disturbing an individual's internal peace. People maintain internal harmony by having a good heart, and a

This picture of leaders of the Hopi villages of Walpi, Hano, and Sichomovi was taken around 1882. While the Hopi traditionally gave all land ownership and much authority to women, political and religious offices were held by men.

good heart is reflected in good deeds and kind thoughts.

But when a Hopi becomes ill, she or he can seek a cure from healers who use a variety of therapies. Some treatments rely on the medicinal properties of natural substances contained in plants and roots. Hopi women and men who are healers know how to make therapeutic teas from numerous wild plants. Patients drink the teas as part of their cure. Healers may also treat illnesses by performing rituals intended to correct imbalances within a patient's heart or mind. Through prayers and appeals to spirits, a patient's good heart can be restored.

The Hopi's way of life helped keep their communities together in peace and harmony for many centuries. Although the Hopi sometimes encountered dangers from environmental conditions such as droughts and from occasional raids by enemies, they were able to survive and maintain their culture. Then in the 16th century, a group of foreign intruders arrived in Hopi territory. These invaders from Spain set off a series of events that brought unforeseen problems to the Hopi and their neighbors. However, despite the onslaught, first by Spanish and later by American forces, the Hopi have been remarkably successful at withstanding foreign domination. Even though they have modified their culture somewhat, they have largely kept to their ancient values and traditions. ▲

A 1760 Spanish map of New Mexico. The Spanish came to the Pueblo Indian homeland seeking gold. Because the Hopi lived a great distance from the Spanish strongholds in the New World and had no mineral wealth, they were among the Indian tribes least affected by the Spanish.

FACING
THE
INTRUDERS

The first European intruders into Pueblo territory were Spanish soldiers and missionaries who ventured north from their bases in Mexico in the early 16th century. After they had defeated and plundered the rich Aztec empire in central Mexico, Spanish officials began to look elsewhere for new lands and new peoples to draw into their domain.

In 1539, a Franciscan priest named Marcos de Niza traveled into present-day New Mexico and Arizona. From a distance, he spotted the village of the Zuni. He did not actually visit Zuni nor any other Pueblo settlement but instead returned to Mexico and told fantastic tales of rich cities, golden treasures, and great wealth to be found in these northern lands. When Spanish officials heard the stories, they organized expeditions to explore the region.

The first contingent was led by Francisco Vásquez de Coronado in 1540. He journeyed into Pueblo territory with a large company of several hundred sol-

diers on foot and on horseback. Among the Spanish travelers were a number of priests belonging to the Franciscan order of the Catholic church. They wanted to establish missions in Indian communities and convert the native peoples to Christianity.

Coronado set up headquarters in a Hopi pueblo called Tiguex near present-day Bernadillo, New Mexico. He remained there for two years. During that time, Coronado sent expeditions to visit other pueblos along the Rio Grande and also sent explorers to the Hopi's western settlements. Pedro de Tovar led a group of 20 soldiers and one Catholic priest to make contact with residents of the prominent Hopi village of Awatovi.

At first, the natives welcomed the Spaniards. They traded with the newcomers and obtained metal tools and utensils from them. The Spanish were given food and clothing by the Pueblo. But Spaniards began to demand more and more goods from the people. The

49

residents of Tiguex soon resented the Spaniards' demands and tried to expel them from the village. The revolt was unsuccessful because the Pueblo's bows and arrows were no match for the Spaniards' guns. Not content with putting down the native uprising, Coronado ordered several hundred Tiguex residents to be executed in retaliation for the uprising. The example of Spanish brutality against defenseless people was quickly told among all the Pueblo.

Thereafter, the Pueblo no longer looked upon the Spanish as friendly visitors but as potential threats.

The Pueblo's worst fears of Spanish intentions came to pass throughout the 16th and 17th centuries. Although the Pueblo Indians in the eastern villages along the Rio Grande suffered the most at the hands of the Spanish, the Hopi were also burdened by Spanish demands for goods and labor. To force the Hopi to do their will, the Spanish

Francisco Coronado leads a party of soldiers and priests into Pueblo territory in 1540. Though Coronado was greatly disappointed not to discover gold, his expedition marked the beginning of the Spanish presence in the Southwest.

lashed them with whips and brutally killed them in summary executions.

A number of expeditions were sent from Mexico to make further inroads into Pueblo territory. In 1582, Antonio de Espejo led a large group of soldiers and missionaries into the region. They traveled throughout the area, visiting Hopi villages in the west and other pueblos in the east. Judging from the Spaniards' own accounts, it seems that Espejo and his men were just as cruel as Coronado had been. For example, one of Espejo's companions, Diego Pérez de Luxán, described an incident that occurred in a town when the Spanish entered and demanded food and other provisions. Since the residents had heard about the Spanish from other Pueblo, they refused the foreigners' requests. In response, according to Luxán,

> the corners of the pueblo were taken by four men, and four others began to seize those natives who showed themselves. And as the pueblo was large and the majority had hidden themselves, we set fire to the big pueblo, where we thought some were burned to death because of the cries they uttered. We at once took out prisoners, two at a time, and lined them up, where they were shot many times until they were dead. Sixteen were executed, not counting those who burned to death.

In the late 16th century, the Spanish government embarked on a new policy. Instead of simply sending expeditions to explore Pueblo territory, they decided to establish permanent colonies of Spanish settlers in the region. Juan de Oñate led the first group of colonizers into New Mexico in 1598. There Oñate set up his base at a Pueblo village, demanding provisions from the inhabitants. Oñate's methods were similar to those employed by Coronado and Espejo. According to accounts written by one of his associates, Oñate

> sent people out every month in various directions to bring maize [corn] from the pueblos. The feelings of the natives against supplying it cannot be exaggerated for they weep and cry out as if they were being killed. The Spaniards seize the blankets by force, leaving the poor Indians stark naked.

Even Spanish authorities in Mexico considered Oñate's activities outrageous. They removed him as governor of the colony in 1607 and appointed a replacement, Pedro de Peralta. Peralta arrived in 1609 and shifted the Spanish headquarters to the pueblo of Santa Fe, which remained the provincial capital throughout the Spanish colonial period.

Unfortunately, Peralta turned out to be no different than his predecessors. He began by forcing the Pueblos in Santa Fe to build a palace and other public buildings for his government. The Spanish compelled Native Americans throughout the province to give them food, blankets, and other goods as tribute. Some Pueblo were enslaved and made to work on farms or in mines and workshops owned by Spaniards; others were forced to serve the Spaniards as domestic servants.

Franciscan missionaries were no better than government authorities or soldiers in their dealings with the Pueblo. They too established large farms and forced the natives to work for them in their fields and homes. Indeed, missionaries often held huge amounts of land that produced much more food than they needed for their own support. They sold the surplus to Spanish officials, soldiers, and settlers and received large profits from this business.

Priests established missions in many Pueblo communities, forcing the residents to erect churches and housing for the missionaries. They ordered all the inhabitants to attend church services and to abandon their traditional religious practices. They also destroyed Pueblo ritual objects and religious works of art.

The Franciscans dealt harshly with the Pueblo, who resisted their attempts to impose the Catholic religion on Native American societies. They meted out public whippings, torture, and even executions as punishments for Pueblo Indians who performed their own ancient rituals.

In 1629, three Franciscans journeyed to Hopi villages and established their first mission at Awatovi, headed by Francisco Porras. Although Porras wanted to convert the Hopi and also demanded their provisions and labor, he was less cruel in his methods than many other missionaries and officials. Porras was somewhat sympathetic toward Hopi people and their culture. For example, he learned to speak the Hopi language in an attempt to communicate directly with them. This was unusual, as most priests spoke only Spanish and used bilingual natives as interpreters. In fact, the heads of Franciscan orders in Mexico and Spain ordered the priests not to learn Indian languages because they were worried that if missionaries spoke directly with the native peoples they might sympathize with the Indians' complaints against Spanish authorities.

In addition to the mission at Awatovi, churches were built in the Hopi villages of Oraibi and Shongopavi. Smaller visitation sites were established in several other towns.

At Awatovi, Porras had some minimal success in converting some of the inhabitants to Catholicism. The Hopi elsewhere showed no interest in the new religion, and even at Awatovi Catholic adherents were in the minority.

However, Franciscans did have far-reaching effects on Hopi life. They introduced the Hopi to many articles of European manufacture. The Hopi especially prized European tools and utensils made of metal, including knives, axes, saws, scissors, and nails. Hopi farmers also began to plant some crops obtained from the Spanish, such as peaches, apples, melons, tomatoes, and chilies. The latter two foods originated among the Aztecs in Mexico but were adopted by Spaniards and taken with them into the Southwest. Finally, the Hopi added sheep and cattle to their native livestock.

By the middle of the 17th century, a

The Roman Catholic church and mission at Acoma, photographed around 1882. Although the Pueblo Indians at Acoma are not Hopi, this church is probably similar to those the Spanish built in the Hopi villages.

series of recurring disasters affected Hopi communities. Severe droughts occurred in the 1640s and 1660s, resulting in crop failures and food shortages. In addition, raids by neighboring Navajo increased during the same period. The Navajo were no doubt affected by the same drought and lost much of their own produce. They therefore turned to raiding Hopi villages in an attempt to obtain food and goods needed for their own survival.

Waves of epidemic diseases such as smallpox and measles struck Hopi settlements in the middle of the 17th century. These diseases were previously unknown among the Hopi, indeed among all Native American communities. Just as particular plants and animals are indigenous to certain areas of the world, organisms that cause diseases also originate in specific regions. Germs causing smallpox and measles were found in Europe but were absent from North and South America before the arrival of Europeans on these continents. Since Native Americans had never been exposed to smallpox and measles, they had not developed any natural immunity or resistance to the diseases. The result was that when the Hopi and other natives first encountered the germs, they succumbed to them in enormous numbers. In some cases, all the members of a household died in the epidemics. Few, if any, families were untouched.

The combination of droughts, raids, and epidemics severely undermined the stability of Hopi society in the 17th century. Many Hopi sought the cause of their misfortunes and found it in the Spanish. The Hopi believed that the balance and harmony of their universe had been disturbed by the foreigners' arrival. Seen from the Hopi's point of view, the Spanish not only had demanded crops, goods, and labor from them but had also overturned the delicate relationships between humans and the natural world that are vital to life and happiness. By attempting to destroy the Hopi religion, missionaries had violated sacred bonds between the Hopi, their ancestors, and their spiritual protectors.

The Hopi often reacted to Spanish abuses by outwardly conforming to their demands. They knew that resistance was futile and would result in brutal retaliation. Sometimes, though, actions by local Spaniards were too outrageous to be ignored. For instance, in 1655, a Hopi delegation traveled to Santa Fe to lodge a complaint with the Spanish governor against a priest in one of their villages who had arrested a leader of a Hopi ritual society. The priest had the man whipped, doused with hot oil, and set on fire. Spanish officials listened to the charges but, as usual, took no steps to punish the priest nor to end the repeated abuses.

After living under Spanish control for more than a century and a half, the Pueblo people finally could endure no more demands and outrages. In 1680, Pueblo leaders began to meet together in secret to devise a plan to rid themselves of the intruders. Most prominent among the leaders was a man named Pope (Po-PAY), a member of a Pueblo

Interior view of the Roman Catholic church at Acoma, which dates from the 17th century.

tribe known as the Tewa. Pope was from the village of San Juan, located near the Rio Grande in New Mexico, and had himself been a victim of Spanish cruelty in 1675, being one of a group of ritual leaders publicly whipped by Spanish authorities for allegedly engaging in witchcraft.

Pope and leaders from all of the Pueblo tribes decided to stage a rebellion against the Spanish in an effort to drive them from the region. After many meetings, the leaders decided on a plan of action that would begin by laying siege to the provincial headquarters in Santa Fe. They wanted to time their attack to occur during the summer of 1680 because they knew that at that time the Spanish would be awaiting new shipments of goods from Mexico, and therefore their supplies of guns and ammunition would be low. Pope and the others thought that the Spanish would surrender and leave the area if they realized that they were cut off from receiving further foods and provisions.

In addition to a siege of Santa Fe, the plan called for participation by all Pueblo communities. Leaders agreed that residents of all the pueblos would attack the Spanish officials, soldiers, and priests who resided in their villages. They set August 11, 1680, as the date for the uprising. Two messengers were chosen to relay the final plan to each pueblo. However, by some means, the Spanish governor, Antonio de Otermin, found out about the impending revolt. On August 9, he arrested the two messengers. When word of the arrests spread in the pueblos, Pope and the other leaders decided to implement their plan immediately. The Pueblo Revolt, as it is called, began on August 10. The most concerted attacks occurred in Rio Grande villages. The rebels successfully cut off water and supplies to Santa Fe and routed nearby Spanish settlers. Soldiers and priests were killed. Otermin finally realized that his forces were unable to defeat the Pueblo and ordered a retreat from Santa Fe on August 21.

Although the Hopi were distant from the New Mexican villages, they too participated in the rebellion. They killed the five priests living in their villages and destroyed the churches that they had previously been forced to build.

Once Spanish settlers, priests, and soldiers began to retreat from Pueblo territory, the natives ceased their attacks. They allowed the foreigners to depart without further incident. Pueblo behavior was thus vastly different from the brutal retaliations that Spanish authorities had often meted out to the native nations.

Peace lasted only for a short 12 years. In 1692, Diego de Vargas led an army back to Pueblo land and successfully imposed control in most of the villages. He and his soldiers executed hundreds of Pueblo resisters and defenseless villagers. Vargas visited Hopi settlements, planning to regain dominance there too. But after the revolt of 1680, the Hopi had moved their villages from the open desert to the tops of three mesas located within their territory. Since the mesas were compact areas and had only one path leading up to the top, the Hopi knew that they could easily spot invaders and block their ascent to the villages.

The Hopi were correct. Vargas tried to attack them but failed to enter their towns. The Hopi were helped by groups of Navajo and Ute who raided the Spanish soldiers.

Spanish authorities sent additional expeditions into Hopi territory with the aim of either convincing the Hopi to submit to Spanish control or forcing them to do so. Both plans failed repeatedly, and Hopi communities successfully withstood foreign domination. They were aided by a number of immigrants

Captain-General Diego de Vargas, governor of New Mexico, reconquered the Southwest for the Spanish after the 1680 revolt. When he visited Hopi territory, he met with a hostile reception everywhere except Awatovi. Many Pueblo Indians who fled the Spanish reconquest sought refuge among the Hopi.

from other Pueblo communities in New Mexico who sought refuge among the western Hopi. The largest group of refugees arrived from the Tewa pueblos in 1696. They took up permanent residence on First Mesa, the easternmost of the three Hopi mesas. The Tewa village, called Hano, shared First Mesa with the Hopi towns of Sichomovi and Walpi.

Franciscan priests made several more attempts to regain a foothold in Hopi towns during the 1690s. Only the residents of Awatovi allowed the priests to set up a mission in their town. All other Hopi were strongly opposed to the priests. They objected to the missionaries' efforts to convert them, and they feared that former demands for labor and the brutal practices of the Spaniards would be forced upon them once again. After failing to convince the people at Awatovi to expel the Franciscans, the Hopi, led by a clan chief named Espeleta, attacked the village in 1701. They killed all the men and forced the women and children to leave the village. Later that year, the Spanish governor in Santa Fe sent an army against the Hopi to punish them for sacking the Catholic mission at Awatovi, but his soldiers were defeated by the Hopi.

Throughout the 18th century, Spanish authorities made occasional attempts to reimpose control over Hopi communities. Expeditions were sent in 1707, 1716, 1775, and 1780. The Hopi, however, were steadfast in their refusal to allow the Spaniards to enter their villages.

With the Pueblo Revolt of 1680, the

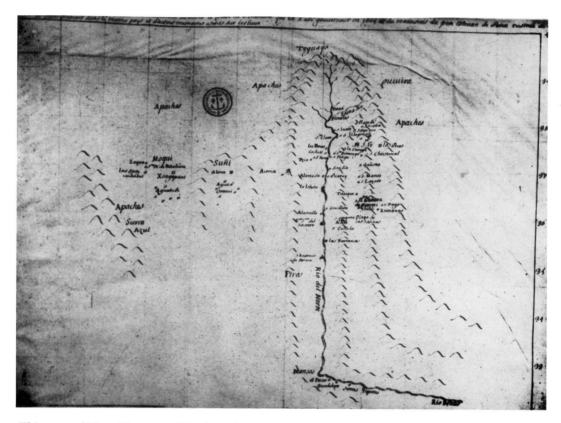

This map of New Mexico, which dates from approximately 1680, shows various Indian tribes and many Pueblo Indian settlements. On this map the Hopi are called "Moqui," the Navajo name for the Hopi.

Hopi had finally been able to rid themselves of Spanish domination. They were successful for several reasons. First, Hopi warriors used their military skills and planning to defend their communities. Second, since Hopi settlements were distant from the center of Spanish colonization in New Mexico, Spanish expenses required to mount repeated campaigns against the Hopi proved excessive. Because of the expense, the Spanish could not maintain continual pressure against the Hopi. Third, the Navajo, Apache, and Ute who lived in the area between the Hopi and the Spanish colonies attacked Spanish soldiers on their way to Hopi territory. Because of the Hopi's defensive strength and favorable external circumstances, the Hopi were able to safeguard their communities and to maintain their culture in relative stability.

Freed from Spanish demands for produce and labor, the Hopi once again devoted their time to traditional pursuits and even experienced an economic recovery in the 18th century. As described by Silvestre Velez de Escalante, a Franciscan traveler to Hopi territory in 1775, the Hopi "are very civilized, apply themselves to weaving and cultivating the land by means of which they raise abundant crops of maize, beans, and chile. They also gather cotton."

Although the Hopi population had declined since the mid-1600s because of disease and warfare, by the middle of the 18th century, Hopi communities had begun to increase again. In 1742, for instance, a Spanish visitor put the number of Hopi at 10,846. This figure probably represents a decline from their aboriginal population but an increase over the previous century.

Still, environmental and external conditions continued to adversely affect Hopi villages from time to time. Several years of severe drought set in beginning in 1777, resulting in crop failures and famine. During the same period, the Hopi were the victims of Navajo raids. Because of these difficulties, approximately 150 Hopi decided to leave their towns and seek aid and relief from the Pueblo in New Mexico. Soon afterward, when the rains came and the crisis lessened, most of the refugees returned to their own villages.

Once again, the Hopi regained their economic stability. They lived according to their traditional way of life, honoring their ancestors and the spirit beings who they believed protected them. Free again to follow their ancient ideals of harmony and balance, the Hopi felt satisfied that they had stayed true to their own way of life. ▲

Lololoma, chief of Oraibi, was originally deeply antagonistic toward the government of the United States. He reversed his attitude in 1875, probably because he was impressed by what he had seen on a trip to Washington, D.C., that same year.

CHALLENGES
TO
HARMONY

The 19th century began for the Hopi as a time of economic and spiritual recovery. Because of their isolation from centers of colonial control, they were able to turn their energies to producing crops and maintaining their households. And they devoted their hearts and minds to honoring the spirit world. But as the century wore on, new intruders entered Hopi territory and challenged their stability and peace.

The Spanish colonies of New Mexico and Arizona came under the control of the Republic of Mexico when it gained its independence from Spain in 1821. Although Mexico had jurisdiction over its northern provinces from that year until the end of the Mexican-American War in 1848, the Pueblo living in New Mexico had little contact with government authorities. The Hopi in Arizona were totally ignored by the Mexicans.

Several factors contributed to the Hopi's continued isolation. First, their history of strong resistance to foreign domination led Mexican officials to leave them in peace. Second, the great distance between Hopi territory and centers of government in Mexico made contact costly in terms of time and money. Third, the Hopi's determination to resist efforts to impose Christianity on them meant that even the Franciscan priests did not make serious efforts to establish missions in Hopi villages. Finally, although tens of thousands of Hispanic settlers lived near the Rio Grande Pueblo in New Mexico, few of them ventured west into Hopi territory because they were fearful of raids by the Navajo and Apache who lived in the western region.

The Mexican government changed the official legal status of Native Americans in the former Spanish colonies. Under Spain, the Hopi and other Native Americans had been considered wards of the Crown, but Mexico granted full citizenship to all native peoples. Although the legal change was a positive step on the part of the Mexican government, it had no particular effect on the

Hopi since they had virtually no contact with Mexican authorities.

In the early 19th century, travelers and traders from the United States began to make their appearance in the Southwest, even though the region was part of the country of Mexico. American trappers and merchants ventured into New Mexico and Arizona seeking beaver pelts for the profitable domestic and foreign markets. Santa Fe became a major regional trading center after 1822, when the Santa Fe Trail was opened. The trail linked the Southwest to the eastern United States and attracted an influx of American traders and settlers throughout the rest of the 19th century.

The Hopi, however, remained isolated from trading activity and from interaction with the new intruders. Still, sporadic contact did take place. Although such contact was generally peaceful, conflict also occurred. In one incident, a group of trappers employed by the Rocky Mountain Fur Company looted Hopi farms in 1840. When the Hopi approached the trappers, they were attacked, and between 15 and 20 Hopi were killed.

After the defeat of Mexico in the Mexican-American War, the territory in which the Pueblo Indians lived became part of the United States under the 1848 Treaty of Guadalupe Hidalgo. American government officials, settlers, and travelers began to arrive in ever-greater numbers. Predictably, as their presence increased, competition over land increased as well. The Hopi and other Pueblo were naturally concerned that the American intruders would encroach on native land. In the Treaty of Guadalupe Hidalgo, the United States had pledged to respect the land rights of all former citizens of Mexico, including the Pueblo. But the legal status of the Pueblo in the United States put them in some jeopardy, for whereas the Pueblo had been citizens under the Mexican state, the United States government did not grant citizenship to native peoples but rather considered them wards of the state. As wards, or legal minors, the Pueblo did not have equal legal standing with Anglo and Hispanic residents. They therefore had to depend on the American government to protect their rights. Unfortunately, such protection was not reliable.

In a move to assert American jurisdiction in the Southwest, the federal Bureau of Indian Affairs (BIA) appointed an agent to deal with Indians in the area. The bureau had been established in 1824 with the duty of overseeing government policies and programs in Native American communities in the United States. The Southwest agent, John Calhoun, set up regional headquarters for the BIA in Santa Fe in 1850. In October of that year, the Hopi sent a delegation of their leaders to meet with Calhoun. The group was headed by a man named Nakwaiyamtewa, who was a clan leader from the village of Oraibi, then the principal Hopi town. Nakwaiyamtewa and the other Hopi representatives had two goals in mind. First, they wanted to establish friendly relations with the new government administra-

Fort Defiance, Arizona, was built in 1851 to protect the region from Navajo raids. One year earlier, a Hopi delegation had traveled to Santa Fe, New Mexico, to ask the U.S. government for help in defending their villages from the Navajos.

tors. Second, they sought help from the Americans in fending off raids by the Navajo and the Ute, which had become more frequent in the early 19th century.

Calhoun was sympathetic toward the Hopi's requests and presented them with gifts as tokens of friendship. He told the Hopi that the Americans would come to their aid. In 1851, the government built a fort, called Fort Defiance, in western New Mexico from which troops were dispatched to fight Navajo and Ute

raiders. Although these expeditions helped protect the Hopi, they were of equal benefit to the growing number of Anglo settlers whose farms and ranches were also targets of raids.

After the establishment of Fort Defiance, American officials visited Hopi villages in 1851 and 1852 in order to meet with Hopi leaders and to observe conditions in the settlements. These visits were followed by a number of disastrous events. A new wave of smallpox epidemics struck the Hopi in 1853 and 1854, resulting in the deaths of hundreds of people. During the same period, serious droughts occurred, further reducing the population through widespread famine. The population of Oraibi, for instance, declined from approximately 800 to only 200 in just a few years.

Further droughts and outbreaks of smallpox hit the Hopi beginning in 1864. Hopi leaders sought relief from American officials but received little aid. As a result, many Hopi left their towns and took temporary refuge among the Zuni. As droughts and disease repeatedly struck their villages, the Hopi population fluctuated throughout the 19th century. Estimates put the total number of Hopi at between 2,000 and 3,000 during the century.

During the American Civil War (1861–65), the American government used its resources to fight the war and therefore devoted little time or material to Indian tribes in the Southwest. Given this situation, raids by the Navajo and the Ute against the Hopi and other Pueblo tribes increased. The raids finally ceased after 1864 when the United States began a brutal policy aimed at controlling the Navajo. The American military was sent to fight the Navajo, killing hundreds, perhaps thousands, of Navajo men, women, and children. Eight thousand Navajo were arbitrarily rounded up by American soldiers and imprisoned at Bosque Redondo, a New Mexico army base. They were held there for four years, from 1864 until 1868. Although the policy restored some measure of

security to the Hopi, it resulted in the deaths of many defenseless Navajo and the destruction of their crops and livestock.

Beginning in the second half of the 19th century, several Christian sects undertook missionary activity among the Hopi. Mormons based in Utah began visiting Hopi settlements in 1858. They set up a mission in 1875 at the village of Moenkopi (MO-en-ko-pi; "flowing-stream place"), a relatively new settlement outside Oraibi. In 1870, another Protestant denomination, the Moravians, established a mission at Oraibi. Baptist and Mennonite missionaries also visited and preached among the Hopi during the same period.

Despite the influx of missionaries, none had any particular success in converting the Hopi. Other changes, however, began to take place, the combined effect of which did change Hopi life. The BIA opened a Hopi Indian Agency at Oraibi in 1870. Four years later, a second agency was established in a nearby town called Keams Canyon, which had been built by a family of Anglo traders. Keams Canyon began as a trading post and later grew into a regional BIA administrative center. Increasing numbers of Anglo immigrants arrived in the area. Some were government employees, others were ranchers, merchants, missionaries, and teachers.

During the 1870s, construction of railroads linking the east and west coasts of the United States brought still more workers and settlers into the Southwest. One line, the Atchison, Topeka, and

(continued on page 73)

SPIRITS AND GODS

For the Hopi, everything in the world—a plant or a bird, the wind or a human being—has a spirit. The Hopi way is to strive for a peaceful and harmonious existence by honoring the spirits of all beings, thereby entering into the right relationship with these spirits and making the world harmonious, balanced, and peaceful. This belief explains the supreme importance in Hopi culture of kachinas, who are regarded as the manifestations of spirits.

Kachinas often visit the Hopi, particularly during important religious ceremonies. On those occasions, the kachinas sometimes leave gifts for the Hopi children. The most special of these gifts are dolls made in the images of the kachinas, which are considered to be a form of the spirit itself. The children's parents take the dolls home and hang them up so that the children may always see them and learn to recognize the kachinas.

Whether kachinas appear as hilarious and outrageous clowns or as the extravagantly beautiful butterfly kachinas, they are all powerful spirits and deities who make the Hopi feel that they are communing with a reality that lies behind and sustains the everyday, visible world.

This Hopi kachina doll represents Avatshoya. A kachina might be named after the animal or spirit it represents, the kind of noise it makes, the way it moves, or some other aspect of its character.

Kuwan Powamu Koyemsi is a Kooyemsi, or mudhead kachina. No one knows exactly how many different kachinas there are in Hopi religious belief, particularly because certain kachinas appear only in certain villages.

Mastopkatsina would visit Oraibi during
Soyalangw, the ceremony that marked
the winter solstice, or as the Hopi said,
the return of the sun to its winter house.
Many of the rituals performed during
Soyalangw are concerned with fertility
and preparations for the upcoming
planting season.

Pawiki is a duck kachina.

67

Tsorporyaqahontaqa (with the blue face) and Eewero are kipokkatsinam, *or raider kachinas. At the end of Hopi dances, the* kipokkatsinam *punish the* tsuskut, *or Hopi clowns, for their un-Hopi-like behavior.*

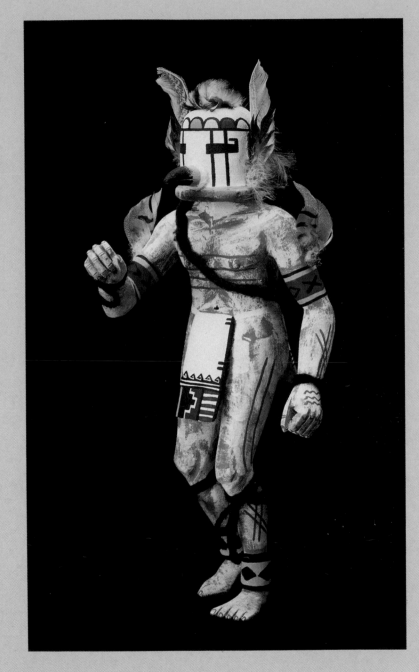

Kisa is a prairie falcon kachina.

Hilili is a kachina doll carved in a simple, traditional style. Traditional kachinas were carved from the root of a cottonwood tree. The Hopi call kachinas carved in this style ponotutuyqa, *or one with a stomachache, referring to the arms clasped over the belly.*

Kweo, the wolf kachina.

Nata'aska is a black ogre kachina. During the Powamuy, or Bean Dance, ceremony, such ogres go from house to house reciting the misdeeds of the children who live within and threatening to kidnap or eat them.

The town of Flagstaff, Arizona, as seen in 1883, almost immediately after its founding. For most of the next century Flagstaff would exert a major influence on the Hopi, as traders, teachers, and tourists used it as a jumping-off point for journeys to the Hopi villages.

(continued from page 64)

Santa Fe, ran about 75 miles south of Hopi territory. When the railroad was completed in 1881, travelers sometimes stopped off and decided to stay in the region. Anglo towns such as Flagstaff, Winslow, and Holbrook were founded. All were no more than 70 miles from Hopi villages. In addition, in 1878 Mormons built their town of Tuba City just to the west of the Hopi mesas. They gradually encroached on Hopi land by expanding their farms and livestock ranges.

The Hopi soon became alarmed at the growing population of Anglos residing in and near their territory. They appealed to American officials for protection against encroachments on their land and harm to their property. In response, President Chester A. Arthur signed an executive order in 1882 that transformed Hopi lands into a protected reservation. The reserved land consisted of two and a half million acres in an area 55 by 70 miles wide. According to the wording of the executive order, the reservation was to be inhabited by "Hopis and other Indians." This wording has recently become extremely significant in disputes between the Hopi and the Navajo over land rights, as we shall see in the next chapter.

Hopi Indians who opposed the U.S. government's attempts to change traditional Hopi ways were known as Hostiles. These Hostiles were photographed in 1895 while imprisoned at Alcatraz for opposing legislation that would have destroyed the Hopi system of land ownership, changing it from clan to individual possession.

Despite increased contact between the Hopi and Anglo newcomers to the region, the Hopi way of life remained essentially unchanged, although some innovations were made. The Hopi adopted some new equipment into their farming technology, including such items as plows, iron hoes, and shovels.

They produced their traditional crops of corn, beans, and squash, adding a few foods borrowed from Europeans. These consisted mainly of fruits such as peaches, apples, and melons. The Hopi also began to use wooden doors and glass windows in their houses, although their architecture and village plans followed traditional patterns. In general, the Hopi people prospered in the late 19th century. While the Hopi continued to adopt some items from Anglo culture that they considered advantageous, they did not abandon their own way of life nor change their ancient values.

Then in the late 1870s and 1880s, a new government policy began to affect the Hopi. Schools were opened for Hopi children, first at Keams Canyon in 1874 and later in Hopi villages. Some Hopi leaders were willing to have the children attend school, but they also voiced concern over the future of Hopi traditions. In 1886, 20 religious leaders sent a letter to the BIA in Washington, D.C., stating that they wanted their children to "learn the American's tongue and their ways of work. [But] we pray that the children may follow in their parents' footsteps and grow up good of heart and pure of breath."

Other Hopi strongly opposed sending their children to Anglo schools. They were concerned that the children would be taught to follow a way of life vastly different from their traditional culture. They feared that the stability and harmony of their existence were threatened by American educational policies. School officials first tried to entice parents to enroll their children by giving them an ax, shovel, or rake as a present. When this tactic failed, authorities arrested Hopi fathers who kept their children at home. The fathers were sentenced to 90 days of hard labor.

In addition, the government sometimes sent soldiers to Hopi villages to round up children and forcibly take them to school. In one particularly disturbing incident that occurred in 1890, soldiers entered a kiva during an initiation rite for boys, disrupted the ceremony, and took all of the boys away.

The Hopi's resentment of the government naturally increased as a result of such actions. Adding to the people's anger, teachers and missionaries criticized Hopi religious practices, which Anglos considered pagan or uncivilized. They convinced government authorities to try to stop the Hopi from performing native rituals. At this time, the United States did not feel that the guarantee of religious liberty in the Constitution extended to Native Americans. The Hopi responded to this interference in their religious life by conducting their ceremonies in secret. Still, the government's policies fueled their bitterness about Anglo interference.

Throughout the last years of the 19th century and the early years of the 20th, two opposing factions developed in Hopi communities. One group strongly opposed Anglo intervention in native life. They were alarmed by encroachments on their land by settlers, farmers, and ranchers. They viewed the influx of Anglo traders, missionaries, government workers, and teachers as a threat to their own survival. And they resented the fact that the government imposed policies on them without any prior consultation.

The other faction favored cooperation with federal and local authorities. They believed that education was advantageous and would lead to prosperity for the Hopi. Many of these people were bilingual and had personal interactions with Anglos through work and casual contact.

Controversies between the two factions worsened by the end of the 19th century. People belonging to the opposing groups, dubbed the Hostiles and the Friendlies in terms of their attitudes toward the American government, disagreed about many issues. The Hostiles opposed all government policies while the Friendlies often cooperated with official programs. For instance, in the late 1890s, when an outbreak of smallpox hit the village of Shongopovi, Hostiles stopped American health workers from entering the town to vaccinate residents and fumigate their houses. The Friendlies at Shongopovi were in favor of the American plan and were angered at the Hostiles' resistance. After heated arguments between the two groups, the Friendlies forced the Hostiles to leave the village.

The Hostiles expelled from Shongopovi were offered refuge by sympathizers in nearby Oraibi. But this move only worsened an already tense situation in Oraibi. People there had long disagreed over whether to send their children to school. This issue became a focus in Oraibi after 1890. In that year, the leader of the Oraibi Friendlies, an influential clan chief named Lololoma, accepted a government invitation to travel to Washington, D.C., in order to consult with officials there. Lololoma and the chiefs of four other villages who

accompanied him were impressed by what they saw and heard in Washington. They returned to their homes, advocating education and other changes in Hopi life. When Lololoma died in 1900, he was succeeded as leader of the Friendlies faction by a young chief named Tewaquaptewa. The Hostiles, led by a chief named Yokeoma, continued their opposition to schools and other government policies.

When the Hostiles from Shongopovi arrived in Oraibi, people there disagreed about whether to accept the refugees. The factions in Oraibi, led by Tewaquaptewa and Yokeoma, each mustered support from their own lineages and clans. After a while, antagonism between the two factions was so strong that the people could no longer interact with each other. The groups even began to hold their ceremonies in separate kivas. This development was particularly striking in the context of Hopi life. The Hopi had always believed that community rituals were essential to maintaining the strength and solidarity of their villages. Harmony and balance in the universe were therefore threatened when the Hostiles and the Friendlies conducted separate ceremonies.

Village leaders finally realized that all attempts to reach a consensus or compromise were futile. They decided that one faction would have to leave Oraibi in order for peace to be restored. But neither group wanted to leave. So the leaders devised a plan that would force one of the factions out. They said that followers of the two groups should

Chief Tewaquaptewa, leader of the Friendlies faction, opposed allowing Hostile refugees from Shongopovi to settle in Oraibi.

Shelters erected by the Hostiles at the encampment that became Hotevilla, the new village founded after the Hostiles were expelled from Oraibi.

engage in a tug-of-war to decide who would stay in Oraibi and who would leave.

The competition was held on September 8, 1906. Hostiles and Friendlies massed on either side of a line drawn on the ground: each side grabbed onto a rope strung across the line, then each and every Hopi in Oraibi pulled with all the might they could muster. The Hos- tiles lost. As a result, their group, numbering 298 people, left Oraibi and set up a new village seven miles away. The village, called Hotevilla (HO-te-vee-la; "juniper slope"), is nestled at the foot of Third Mesa. The Friendlies, 324 in number, remained in their natal town.

At the end of the bitter conflict, a young Hopi man named Robert Selena wrote an inscription on a large boulder marking the line drawn on the earth of Oraibi for the tug-of-war. The inscription read:

> Well it have to be done
> This way now
> That when you pass me over the line
> It will be done
> September 8, 1906

The events at Oraibi show how the Hopi deal with crises. When disagreements first arose, people talked about the issues and tried to convince others to see their point of view. After a while, though, the dispute deepened, and members of each group began to avoid contact with those in the other faction.

Such avoidance even led to the separation of religious ceremonies. Finally, when village leaders realized that the people would never be able to agree, they knew that the community could no longer function as a harmonious unit. Without harmony, life was impossible. Leaders also feared that prolonging the dispute might lead to physical violence between opposing groups. The tug-of-war was thus a way of resolving the problem without bloodshed.

By separating their communities, both factions hoped to be able to reestablish harmony in their own villages and to resume their lives in peace. The 20th century, however, has proven to be a time of change for all peoples. ▲

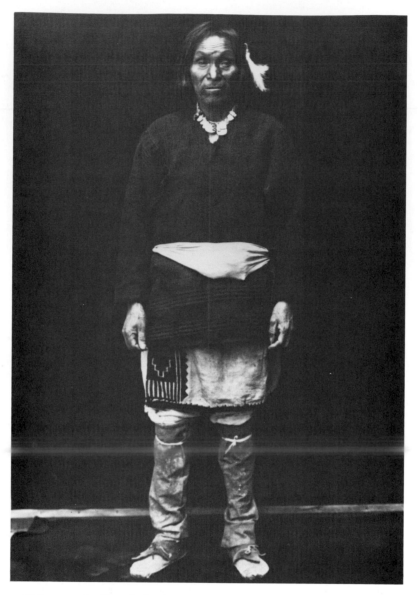

Yokeoma, the Hostile leader and founder of Hotevilla, was photographed in Washington, D.C., in 1910, where he was sent to meet President Taft in the hope that the encounter would make him more willing to give up traditional Hopi ways. The president was famous for his corpulence, but, wrote Hopi Indian agent Leo Crane, "not even the size of President Taft impressed the old spider-like Hopi prophet."

6

ADJUSTING TO CHANGE

While it is possible to see the conflict at Oraibi in September 1906 as a failure of the Hopi to reconcile their differences, it is important to remember that the root cause of the disagreement was the United States government's desire, however well intentioned, to control the Hopi. Although the Hopi had resolved the immediate crisis—albeit at a high price—the problem of not having control over their lives would continue to plague them for the remainder of the century.

Immediately after the Hostiles left Oraibi in September 1906 and moved to Hotevilla, American authorities began to exert control over the new Hopi community. Leaders of the Hostiles, including Yokeoma and other clan chiefs, were arrested and imprisoned at Fort Wingate.

One of the main irritants between the Hopi and the U.S. government continued to be the issue of education. The government chose to focus its energies on education because it believed that if Hopi children were taught in schools, they would eventually abandon their own cultural traditions and follow instead the American way of life.

To accomplish this goal, schools for Hopi children were set up in Keams Canyon rather than in native villages. This forced the children to live where the schools were and separated them from their families. Every effort was made to strip them of their own culture and to impose American culture in its place. Their Hopi clothing was taken away, and they were forced to wear Anglo-style clothing. They were forced to attend Christian religious classes and participate in church services. Finally, they were even forbidden to speak the Hopi language. Children caught speaking Hopi, whether in classrooms, playgrounds, or dormitories, were slapped or whipped.

Yokeoma and some of his supporters on their way to prison after being arrested in 1915 for their refusal to let Hopi children attend American schools. While in prison, Yokeoma told Leo Crane, who had ordered his arrest, "I shall go home sometime. . . . White men come to the Desert, and white men leave the Desert; but the Hopi, who came up from the Underworld, remain."

So intent was the government on carrying out its policy of supplanting Hopi culture with American that force was used. Soldiers arrived in Hotevilla, rounded up all of the children, and took them to the Keams Canyon school under military escort. In the autobiography of Helen Sekaquaptewa, a Hopi woman who was eight years old at the time, the author relates how the children reacted to their predicament:

> Evenings we would gather in a corner and cry softly so that the matron would not hear and scold or spank us. I can still hear the plaintive little voices saying "I want to go home. I want my mother."

Although schoolchildren from most Hopi villages were allowed to return home for summer vacations, boys and girls from Hotevilla were kept in school all year round. The forced separation of Hotevilla parents and children was both a punishment for the parents' objections to government policies and an attempt to wean the children away from their own traditions.

Instead of spending their summers at home, speaking their native language, and participating in Hopi religious life, children from Hotevilla worked in the homes of Keams Canyon's Anglo residents. Government officials, ministers, and traders contracted with the schools for the children's services. Girls carried out domestic tasks such as cleaning and cooking while boys ran errands and did manual work around the house.

Hopi men who continued to object to the government's actions were arrested and jailed in Keams Canyon. In all, 70 men were sentenced for up to one year of hard labor. Helen Sekaquaptewa noted that she frequently saw her father and the other prisoners walk past the schoolyard on their way to the labor camp. She commented:

> They were fastened together in twos with ball and chain. They were not ashamed of their condition because they knew in their hearts they had done nothing wrong; they had only protested having their lives interfered with.

Over the next few years, the government expanded its educational program by opening day schools in Shongopavi and other villages. Again, many parents did not want to send their children to school; again, soldiers arrived to escort the children. And as before, the men who objected were arrested and imprisoned.

Since the schools in Keams Canyon and the Hopi villages only provided education through the sixth grade, older children were sent out of the region to other schools. Most teenagers attended either the Phoenix Indian School in Phoenix, Arizona, the Haskell Institute in Oklahoma, or the Sherman Indian School in Riverside, California. In addition to offering academic and vocational classes, these schools organized work programs for students in the summertime. Teenagers were hired by agricultural businesses to work as farm laborers

The school at Keam's Canyon where Hopi children were forced to endure separation from their families. While the Hopi saw the enforced education as a great cruelty, the Bureau of Indian Affairs agents believed that they were rescuing children from a state of savagery.

on plantations in Colorado and California.

Then, in 1939, the first Hopi high school was opened in the village of Oraibi. After that time, teenagers could complete their education locally rather than having to attend distant boarding schools.

During the early years of the 20th century, the federal government introduced a variety of other programs on the Hopi Reservation. In 1913, a hospital was opened in Keams Canyon for treatment of Hopi and Navajo Indians. Clinics staffed by nurses and doctors on a rotating basis were started in some of the villages. Other government projects addressed economic conditions on the

Hopi Reservation. In an attempt to improve agricultural production, the government provided funds for drilling wells and for building irrigation ditches and flood-control dikes. Finally, in response to an outbreak of skin disease among the sheep owned by Hopi herders, a program of sheep-dipping was started in the the late 1920s. Once a year, owners of livestock took their sheep to sheep-dips where the animals were washed with a medicinal solution to protect them from infection.

Federal policy toward Native Americans took an important new direction in the 1930s. A few years before that time, a national survey of reservations (the Merriam Report) had documented high levels of poverty, malnutrition, and disease in Native American communities. In response, funds for reservations were increased and efforts were made to address local problems.

After Franklin Delano Roosevelt became president in 1933, he placed John Collier at the head of the BIA. Collier was a man with a deep knowledge of and appreciation for Native Americans, and he genuinely wanted to use the BIA to help them. Under the direction of its new commissioner, the BIA pressed for passage in Congress of the Indian Reorganization Act (IRA). When the IRA was passed in 1934, it provided for a limited degree of self-government on federal Indian reservations. Each community was empowered to adopt a constitution, elect a tribal council, and participate in developing local programs. Although in actual practice local independence was severely restricted, the IRA at least recognized Native American rights to land. It also encouraged continuation of traditional ways of life.

After passage of the IRA, according to the act's provisions, a referendum was held in Hopi villages so that people could express either their support for or opposition to accepting the act's provisions. The overwhelming majority of the Hopi refused to participate in the referendum. By staying away from the vote, most Hopi showed their disapproval of the entire process. But of those who did vote, most favored the IRA. The act then went into effect: a tribal council was elected in 1935, and a formal constitution was adopted the following year.

Even though the IRA was officially accepted, controversies arose within the Hopi community over the issue of community leadership. In a continuation of the two divergent attitudes the Hopi had earlier taken toward cooperation with the American government, this split in opinion found new expression in response to the IRA. One group of Hopi, called the Progressives, supported the system of elected representatives. Another faction, called the Traditionals, wanted to maintain clan chiefs as the legitimate local leaders. Two systems of leadership therefore coexist in Hopi villages.

During the 1930s, the BIA began a program to reduce the amount of livestock owned by Hopi and Navajo herders. The stock-reduction policy was a response to the problem of soil erosion on the reservations. Although John Collier of the BIA genuinely wanted to improve conditions for the Hopi and the Navajo, the program was poorly designed and unfairly implemented. Members of the affected communities were not consulted before the policy was put into effect. The Hopi and the Navajo were shocked and angered when they were told that they would have to surrender up to half of their sheep. When they objected to the program, government officials told them that they had no power to change the policies.

A serious flaw in the program was that although the government paid owners for the sheep they had to surrender, the market price of sheep brought to slaughter did not equal the real value of

the animals. Most Hopi did not ordi-
narily sell their sheep for food but rather
kept them for the wool they produced. If
a sheep is sheared every year, its owner
keeps receiving an income from the sale
of wool. In contrast, if a sheep is sold,
money is only earned once. By paying
herders at the market rate, the government did not actually compensate the
Hopi and the Navajo for the lost lifetime
value of their sheep.

The entire experience of stock reduc-
tion left a permanent mark on relations
between the Hopi and the federal government. It again raised the issue of local
control over community life and well-
being. The Hopi felt that their opinions
and interests had been ignored, and they
saw the program as another example of
government interference.

In 1948, the bureau began another
policy that proved to be unpopular. The
BIA opened the Branch of Relocation,
the goal of which was to relocate Native
Americans from reservations to cities
throughout the United States. Few jobs
were available on or near most reservations, and the relocation program was
an attempt to alleviate the resultant
unemployment. One of the stated intentions of the relocation program was to
help Indians obtain jobs in urban centers. The Branch of Relocation supplied
funds for transportation from reservations to cities and in some cases paid for
job training. But once again, the BIA had
not asked the Hopi or other Native
Americans what they wanted.

Indians from all reservations were
included in the program. The Hopi were
encouraged to enroll and relocate to
such western cities as Phoenix, Arizona;
Denver, Colorado; and Los Angeles,
California. But very few Hopi agreed to
relocate. Most preferred to continue
farming and raising their sheep or to try
to seek jobs in nearby Anglo towns.

In fact, the relocation program
proved to be a dismal failure all over
the United States. Although it officially
aimed at improving economic conditions for Native Americans, most Indians who moved to cities found
themselves jobless and living in
decaying urban ghettos. The large
majority of people who did agree to relocate eventually returned to their reservations, finding that they preferred to live
on their own land and to find emotional
and material support in their own communities.

In 1950, Congress passed the Navajo-
Hopi Act, which allotted a sum of $88
million for improvements on both reservations. The funds paid for the construction of wells, fences, roads, and
flood-control dikes. Although the
money was put to good use, many traditional leaders continued to object to government interference in their lives.

By the middle of the 20th century,
concern grew among many Hopi over
the issue of loss of their original territory. In 1949, 24 traditional leaders sent a
letter to authorities in Washington, D.C.,
expressing their convictions about the
importance of land. They said:

> This land is the sacred home of the
> Hopi people. It was given to the

John Collier, commissioner of the Bureau of Indian Affairs, on a visit to Sells, Arizona.
Collier was an admirer of Native American culture and had a special respect for the Pueblo.

Hopi people the task to guard this land by obedience to our traditional and religious instructions. We have never abandoned our sovereignty to any foreign power or nation.

Hopi leaders appealed to the federal Indian Claims Court, founded in 1946, to investigate Hopi claims to land they considered to be theirs. The suit, filed in 1950, stated that land had been illegally sold from the territory promised to the Hopi in the 1882 executive order that had established the reservation. In addition to the problem of land lost through sales and encroachment by Anglo settlers, another factor contributing to the shrinking of the Hopi's land base grew out of the wording of the 1882 executive order that established the Hopi Reservation. That order set aside land for the "Hopis and other Indians." Among the "other Indians" were Navajo whose territory was adjacent to that of the Hopi. Many Navajo gradually moved onto land located within the borders of the original Hopi Reservation. Since the Navajo population had grown quickly, they sought additional acreage for sheep grazing and farming. The BIA allowed the Navajo to move onto the Hopi lands since this did not violate the original executive order. But the Navajo's presence naturally worried the Hopi, who feared that their rights to land would one day be endangered.

In the 1950s, the Hopi and the Navajo began negotiations over the issue of land rights. Federal authorities became involved and recommended a court review of the problem. In 1962, a panel of three judges granted the Hopi exclusive use of the area consisting of their villages and the immediately surrounding land. This area, called District Six, contained 631,306 acres of the original 2,500,000-acre reservation. In the remaining portion of the Hopi Reservation, the Hopi and the Navajo were given "joint, undivided and equal rights."

The wording of the court's decision was unfortunately just as vague and unsatisfactory as that of the 1882 executive order. By stating that the two groups had "joint and undivided" rights to land, the problem of where people would settle and farm and where they could graze their sheep was not resolved. Joint administration of land by the Hopi and the Navajo proved to be cumbersome and led to conflict. Indeed, conflict over land rights continued to plague the Hopi and the Navajo for many years. In one attempt to solve the problem, the Navajo Tribal Council in 1970 offered to pay the Hopi for outright purchase of the so-called joint-use area in which both Hopi and Navajo lived. This proposal angered the Hopi since it implied that they would be willing to sell their rights to their ancestral territory.

After more controversy and negotiations between the Hopi and Navajo tribes, the federal government again stepped in to resolve the problem. In 1974, Congress passed the Navajo-Hopi Settlement Act which provided for the division of the joint-use area. The act, amended in 1978 and 1988, divided the

Thomas Banyacya, a Hopi Indian, addresses Navajo and Hopi Traditionalists at a 1972 meeting of the Hopi-Navajo Unity Committee. The purpose of the meeting was to organize opposition to the joint-use policy. Others in the photograph are, left to right, Chief Claude (Hopi), Daniel Peaches (Navajo), and Mina Lansa (Hopi).

joint-use area evenly between the two tribes. Each received approximately 911,000 acres for their exclusive use. People who found themselves living on land assigned to the other tribe were given a period of five years to move. The federal government supplied funds for relocation and for purchasing additional land for the Navajo. In general, the Hopi have responded more favorably to the decision than have the Navajo. Since rela-

tively few Hopi were living on land given to the Navajo, few Hopis' lives were disrupted.

In addition to problems over land claims and land use, the Hopi have disagreed over the direction of economic development in their communities. Beginning in 1961, the Hopi Tribal Council agreed to lease land to American companies for production of oil, gas, and minerals. One of the largest projects

Coal being mined at Black Mesa. The three mesas on which the Hopi live are situated on a lower cliff of Black Mesa, so Hopi Traditionalists viewed the mining with great alarm. In the lawsuit they filed in 1971 to stop the mining, the Traditionalists stated that Black Mesa was "part of the heart of our Mother Earth."

was started in 1966 by the Peabody Coal Company. Peabody sought and obtained a lease to carry out strip-mining for coal in Black Mesa. The lease provides that the Hopi tribe receive royalties of $500,000 per year. But many Traditionals strongly opposed the project because they saw it as a violation of their sacred trust to protect their land. Traditionals noted that strip-mining has a very destructive effect on land. Although the Peabody Company prom-

ised to revitalize the land after the end of mining operations, Traditionals did not believe that such pledges were realistic. They also objected to Peabody's plans to use water beneath Black Mesa in their mining procedures. Traditionals knew that water is a precious resource in Hopi territory and feared that Peabody's use would interfere with farming.

As an outgrowth of their concerns, Traditional chiefs from 10 of the 13 Hopi villages filed a suit in 1971 to block Peabody's mining operations. The suit also named the United States Department of the Interior and the BIA as codefendants along with Peabody. The plaintiffs argued that the BIA reneged on its obligations to protect Indian lands and rights. The chiefs' statement in the suit echoed the words of their Hopi forebears regarding the importance of land and tradition: "If the land is abused, the sacredness of Hopi life will disappear."

The Traditionals also claimed that the Hopi Tribal Council had no authority to dispose of Hopi land. Since only a small number of Hopi voted in tribal elections, Traditionals did not acknowledge the council as representative of the Hopi people or of their interests.

Although the legal suit against Peabody was denied, Traditionals believed that it was important to raise the issues of leadership and sovereignty. The Hopi may have different opinions about these topics, but they agree that all people should have the right to decide how to govern themselves and how to conduct their lives. These are ancient values, kept alive by countless generations. ▲

Hopi silversmith Eldon Siewiyumptewa, Sr., solders a piece of overlay. Silversmithing was introduced to the Hopi in 1890 by way of the Navajo. Although in many ways Hopi civilization is very conservative, the Hopi have often welcomed change when they could incorporate new material into their own culture on their own terms.

THE
HOPI
TODAY

The lives of the Hopi people today are, of course, vastly different from those of their ancestors who lived centuries ago. External conditions have changed, but with the possible exception of the Zuni, the Hopi have been able to maintain more of their cultural traditions and values than any other tribe of Native Americans.

The principles of harmony and balance, so important to the strength and survival of Hopi communities, remain as guiding ideals for the people today. In the autobiography of Don Talayesva, a Hopi chief of the Sun clan, he recalls the wise words of his uncle who taught him to respect the ancient ways:

Put your trust in the Cloud People. They come from the six directions to examine our hearts. If we are good, they gather above us in cotton masks and white robes and drop rain to quench our thirst and nourish our plants. Rain is what we need most and when the gods see fit they can pour it on us. Keep bad thoughts behind you and face the rising sun with a cheerful spirit, as did our ancestors in the days of plenty. Work hard, keep the ceremonies, live peaceably, and unite your heart with ours so that our messages will reach the Cloud People. Then maybe they will pity us and drop the rains on our fields.

These words express the timeless values of the Hopi. Still, even for the Hopi, the practical reality of life has changed. Most Hopi no longer support themselves exclusively by the traditional pursuit of farming. Instead, many Hopi gain their livelihood from wagework or from combinations of wages, farming, and raising livestock. Members of a family often pursue different kinds of work, all contributing their share of wages, income, or produce to the household.

Still, farming remains an important element in the Hopi economy. The traditional staples of corn, beans, and squash are still planted and highly prized. In addition, Hopi farmers grow melons, other varieties of fruit, and wheat. Many families keep a stock of sheep, goats, and cattle. They sell wool from the sheep at local markets. Dairy and beef cattle also provide some income.

Hopi families utilize the produce from their farms and livestock in their own households. They may also sell surplus crops and goods at local markets. Trading and selling to nearby Navajo is another source of income for the Hopi.

Since the middle of the 20th century, wagework has increased as a share of the Hopi economy. Various kinds of employment are available in Anglo towns near the reservation. Men often work as construction workers, carpenters, and in other building trades. Women tend to obtain jobs as waitresses, clerks, secretaries, and maids. Still other Hopi find employment in a variety of capacities with the Hopi Tribal Council and federal agencies such as the BIA. Schools, health care facilities, and tribal enterprises provide jobs for a small but growing number of people.

Although many villages maintain their basic traditional plan, some new towns have been founded. These towns reflect changes in Hopi life. For example, the town of Moenkopi began as an outgrowth of the old village of Oraibi in the late 19th century. It has a rather unusual legal status. Although it is a Hopi town, it is located outside of the area designated as the Hopi Reservation by the 1882 executive order. Despite its location, Moenkopi was administered by the BIA's Hopi Agency in Keams Canyon. In 1900, when the boundaries of the Navajo Reservation were set, Moenkopi found itself within Navajo territory. Nonetheless, it remained under the jurisdiction of the Hopi Agency.

Moenkopi residents rely on a mixed economy of farming, sheepherding, and wagework. Although few jobs are available in the town itself, residents seek work in nearby Tuba City, located two miles away. Tuba City was founded by Mormons in the 1870s and has grown to a population of between 2,000 and 3,000. Most of its permanent residents are Navajo, although Hopi and Anglos also live there.

The Hopi in Moenkopi shop in stores and seek services available in Tuba City. They also travel 70 miles away from the reservation to the larger center of Flagstaff for shopping and for employment. Some Hopi attend schools in either Tuba City or Flagstaff. They may also seek medical treatment or other services there.

Although towns like Tuba City and Flagstaff provide some jobs and services for the Hopi, serious economic problems persist for the Hopi Nation. Most businesses are owned by outsiders, especially Anglos. Anglos are also the main providers of services as well as the

Sheep ranching at Third Mesa. Sheep and cattle, which the Hopi acquired from the Spanish, are the major forms of Hopi men's property. The wool clipped from the sheep is sold, and lambs provide meat for important occasions such as weddings and initiations.

administrators employed by government agencies. The Hopi tend to be concentrated in low-paying, unskilled, and temporary jobs.

Another village on the Hopi Reservation that has an unusual history is that of Hano, one of three towns situated on First Mesa. Hano was founded in 1696 by Tewa people who previously had lived in pueblos along the Rio Grande in New Mexico. They had fought against the Spanish in the Pueblo Revolt of 1680.

When the Spanish reconquered New Mexico 12 years later, a group of Tewa decided to leave their homes and resettle among the Hopi in Arizona.

The Tewa and the Hopi have somewhat different accounts of the events that led to the Tewa's arrival at the Hopi mesas in 1696. According to the Hopi, the Tewa asked to join Hopi communities and offered to help protect them against attacks from Spaniards or raids by the Navajo and Ute. The Tewa version of how they came to live among the Hopi is quite different. The Tewa say that the Hopi sent a delegation to the Tewa village in New Mexico to ask the Tewa to come to their aid. The Hopi knew of the Tewa's reputation as skilled warriors and wanted their help in fending off Navajo raids. The Hopi leaders promised to give them a good place to build their houses and much land on which to plant their crops. The Tewa chiefs accepted the offer and led their families westward. When they arrived in Hopi territory, the Hopi refused to allow them into their villages and the Hopi did not treat the Tewa with the respect they had promised but instead insulted and ridiculed them. Finally, after the Tewa defeated a group of Ute raiders who came to raid Hopi fields, Hopi leaders agreed to let the Tewa remain. They gave their protectors a portion of land on First Mesa. The Tewa village of Hano is located at the tip of the Mesa where the road descends to the desert below. It shares First Mesa with two Hopi villages, Sichomovi and Walpi.

The Tewa's story of their arrival in Hopi territory continues with an account of a curse that Tewa leaders put on the Hopi because of the rude treatment they received:

> Our clan chiefs dug a pit between Hano and the Hopi villages on First Mesa and told the Hopi clan chiefs to spit into it. When they had all spat, our clan chiefs spat above the spittle of the Hopis. The pit was refilled, and then our clan chiefs declared: "Because you have behaved in a manner unbecoming to human beings, we have sealed knowledge of our language and our way of life from you. You and your descendants will never learn our language and our ceremonies, but we will learn yours. We will ridicule you both in your language and our own."

Whatever the initial motivation, the Tewa came to live in Hopi territory and built their village at the top of First Mesa in 1696. From this vantage point, they successfully defended First Mesa against enemy intruders. When Spanish soldiers tried to attack the Hopi in the early 18th century, the Tewa helped defeat them.

In one incident that occurred in 1716, a Spanish expedition arrived in Hopi territory to try to convince the Tewa at Hano to return to their Rio Grande pueblos. When the Tewa refused, Spanish soldiers fired on them, killing eight people. As they departed, the Spaniards destroyed the crops in the Tewa's fields.

In addition to defending the community from Spanish armies, the Tewa used

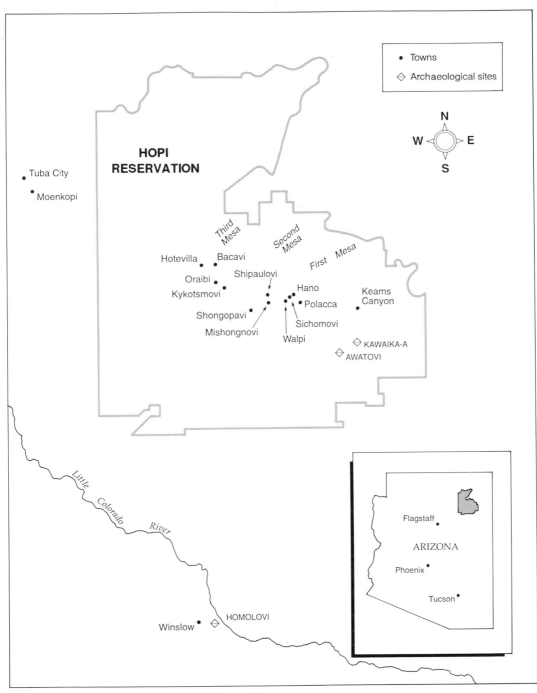

The Hopi reservation.

their military skills to defend First Mesa against Navajo and Ute raiders.

The Tewa and the Hopi have lived near each other on First Mesa since 1696. Despite this geographical proximity, their villages have remained distinct. As an indication of their social separation, the Hopi and the Tewa conduct rituals in their own kivas. Although the Tewa have maintained a strong sense of their unique cultural identity, they have borrowed some Hopi customs. For instance, while the Tewa in New Mexico do not have a strong clan system, those at Hano have adopted matrilineal clans like the Hopi. In addition, like the Hopi, Tewa households are matrilineal.

For two centuries after the Tewa arrived at First Mesa, they and the Hopi did not intermarry. By the beginning of the 20th century, women and men from the two groups occasionally married. Today, approximately half of all Tewa men and women have Hopi spouses. Following the current custom of both peoples, married men move to their wives' households. Although relations between families of an intermarried couple are friendly and cooperative, Hopi men living in Tewa households do not speak the Tewa language. Since all Tewa are bilingual, Tewa men residing among the Hopi speak Hopi, but the Hopi never learn Tewa. The people today are thus living out the curse put on the Hopi by Tewa clan leaders centuries ago.

The course of history of the Tewa at Hano followed a path similar to that of the Hopi. In the 19th and 20th centuries, they faced the same challenges from intruders and from American officials pressuring them to give up their traditional way of life. Since the Tewa had a long history of intermingling with different groups, many of them were quick to learn English. They often served as interpreters between the Hopi and Anglos. As their history had made them adaptable, the Tewa were often more willing than their Hopi neighbors to adopt educational and economic changes introduced by American authorities.

The population of Hano has continued to grow, as has the population of Hopi villages. The three First Mesa towns of Hano, Sichomovi, and Walpi each have approximately 550 residents. A second Tewa village was established at the foot of First Mesa in 1888. It is named Polacca, after its founder, Tom Polacca, who was an influential Tewa leader.

Economic development on the Hopi Reservation is growing, but it is still limited. In the 1970s, the tribe opened a complex consisting of a motel, restaurant, craft shop, and museum. The center, located on Second Mesa, attracts visitors and people interested in purchasing Hopi crafts.

Hopi arts have become quite popular throughout the United States. One specialty is traditional Hopi pottery. Although Hopi women made pottery long ago, the craft died out in the 17th century. Then, in 1900, a woman named Nampeyo from the village of Hano studied ancient earthen bowls, dishes, and jars found in prehistoric Hopi sites. She

Joy Navasie and her grandson Charles paint traditional Hopi pottery, which is known and appreciated worldwide. The Hopi Craft Guild maintains a building on Second Mesa where any Hopi potter, basket maker, weaver, or other artisan can display and sell his or her work.

began to produce pottery using traditional materials and designs. Since then, other Hopi artisans have taken up the craft of pottery. Their work is highly prized.

A number of other Hopi artists, sculptors, and silversmiths have gained recognition for their skills. Among these are the painter Fred Kabotie and silver-smiths Otellie and Charles Loloma. Charles Loloma is famous for his innovative and striking designs in silver, turquoise, and shell jewelry.

Although some Hopi have moved from the reservation to either nearby or distant cities, the population of Hopi villages has increased throughout this century. In 1900, the population was

A Hopi man plants corn. Today, as since time immemorial, the Hopi, whether Traditional or Progressive, realize that land is the key to preserving the Hopi way of life so that it can be passed on to the next generation.

between 2,000 and 2,500. By 1950, the number had risen to approximately 4,400, and by 1980 it had increased to 6,591. Recent population statistics for 1990 indicate a total of 7,360 Hopi living on the reservation. There are slightly more men than women: 3,777 men and 3,583 women. The community is relatively young, having a median age of 26.3 years. There are also a substantial number of elders, totaling 610 individuals who are 65 years of age or older.

Federal statistics on household composition indicate that there are 1,866 housing units occupied on the reservation. Most households (1,468) consist of either a traditional extended group of relatives, a married couple, a couple and their children, or a single parent and children. A small number of houses (231) are occupied by a single person. The proportion of total households consisting of families is higher among the Hopi than among the general American population. This demographic evidence that the Hopi have maintained strong communal and kinship bonds is further proof of the continuity of traditional Hopi values.

The Hopi have managed to endure over four centuries of contact with foreign intruders and have been able to sustain their culture despite strong pressures to adopt Anglo ways. They have lived through many periods of economic and political hardship. Change in Hopi life has occurred, of course, as it has for all other people. But even though many Hopi now work in modern settings, speak English, and participate in local and national political movements, the Hopi philosophy of life is strong and vital. This philosophy teaches the importance of balance and harmony. It stresses the goodness of social bonds among tribal members and the sacredness of spiritual bonds between human beings and all other creatures and forces in the universe.

An eloquent summation of the Hopi religion and of how the Hopi see their dilemma as an ancient culture struggling to exist under the dominion of another, more powerful culture is given in a statement made in 1954 by Andrew Hermequaftewa, the Bluebird Chief of the village of Shongopovi:

> Our religious teachings are based upon the proper care of our land and the people who live upon it. We must not lose this way of life if we are to remain Hopis, The Peaceful.
>
> We were told that if we accept any other way of life we will so bring trouble upon ourselves. Our forefathers told us this, and their forefathers before them. We believe that if you [the United States government] continue with the present policy, our land will be gone and our way of life will be destroyed. You have marvelous intentions; but many of these seem to lead only to destruction of the Hopi Way.
>
> Many things were prophesied to us, and are being fulfilled today. If we foresake our Hopi religion the land will foresake us. There will be no more Hopi Way, no more Hopi people, nor more peace.
>
> We, the Hopi leaders, want to sit with you and consider all these ancient teachings, the advice that has come to us from our ancestors, and the effects upon our way of life of the white man's power that is in Washington. We do not want to see the Hopi Way destroyed.
>
> I ask, as a Hopi, as the Bluebird-Chief, will you in Washington who are in authority come and hold council with us? We would stop this loss of our land and destruction of what we have chosen as our way of life. We want to live as Hopis and worship the way we have been doing since the beginning. The Hopi religion is a way of peace that must be shared with all people. May we so share this with you? That is all. ▲

BIBLIOGRAPHY

Courlander, Harold, ed. *Hopi Voices: Recollections, Traditions, and Narratives of the Hopi Indians.* Albuquerque: University of New Mexico Press, 1982.

————. *The Fourth World of the Hopis: The Epic Story of the Hopi Indians as Preserved in Their Legends and Traditions.* Albuquerque: University of New Mexico Press, 1992.

Dozier, Edward. *Hano: A Tewa Indian Community in Arizona.* New York: Holt, Rinehart & Winston, 1966.

James, Harry Clebourne. *Pages from Hopi History.* Tucson: University of Arizona Press, 1974.

Malotki, Ekkehart. *Hopitutuwutsi or Hopi Tales: A Bilingual Collection of Hopi Indian Stories.* Tucson: University of Arizona Press, 1983.

Mullett, G. M. *Spider Woman Stories: Legends of the Hopi Indians.* Tucson: University of Arizona Press, 1979.

Ortiz, A., ed. *Handbook of North American Indians.* Vol. 9, *The Southwest.* Washington, DC: Smithsonian Institution, 1980.

Simmons, Don. *Sun Chief: The Autobiography of a Hopi Indian.* New Haven: Yale University Press, 1942.

Smith, Watson. *When Is a Kiva? And Other Questions About Southwestern Archaeology.* Tucson: University of Arizona Press, 1990.

Stephen, Alexander MacGregor. *Hopi Journal.* Edited by Elsie Clews Parsons. New York: AMS Press, 1994.

Thompson, Laura, and Alice Joseph. *The Hopi Way.* New York: Russell & Russell, 1965.

Titiev, Mischa. *Old Oraibi: A Study of the Hopi Indians of Third Mesa.* Albuquerque: University of New Mexico Press, 1992.

Udall, Louise. *Me and Mine: The Life Story of Helen Sekaquaptewa.* Tucson: University of Arizona Press, 1969.

Waters, Frank. *The Book of the Hopi.* New York: Penguin Books, 1977.

Whiteley, Peter M. *Deliberate Acts: Changing Hopi Culture Through the Oraibi Split.* Tucson: University of Arizona Press, 1988.

Wright, Barton. *The Unchanging Hopi.* Flagstaff: Northland Press, 1975.

Wyckoff, Lydia L. *Designs and Factions: Politics, Religion, and Ceramics on the Hopi Third Mesa.* Albuquerque: University of New Mexico Press, 1990.

THE HOPI AT A GLANCE

TRIBE   *Hopi*
CULTURE AREA   *Southwest*
GEOGRAPHY   *Northeastern Arizona*
LINGUISTIC FAMILY   *Uto-Aztecan*
CURRENT POPULATION   *7,360*
STATUS   *Tribal Reservation, established in 1882*

GLOSSARY

agent A person appointed by the Bureau of Indian Affairs to supervise U.S. government programs on a reservation and/or in a specific region.

Anasazi Tradition The way of life followed by the ancestors of the Pueblo Indians from around A.D. 1100 until the 14th century; Anasazi people transformed the culture of their ancestors to that of an urban society by creating elaborate systems of water control and building stone houses aboveground, joined to each other, and having entrances in the roofs.

anthropology The study of the physical, social, and historical characteristics of human beings.

Branch of Relocation A Bureau of Indian Affairs program that helps Hopi obtain jobs in urban areas.

Bureau of Indian Affairs (BIA) A federal government agency now within the Department of the Interior. Originally intended to manage trade and other relations with Indians, the BIA now seeks to develop and implement programs that encourage Indians to manage their own affairs and to improve their educational opportunities and general social and economic well-being.

culture The learned behavior of humans; nonbiological, socially taught activities; the way of life of a group of people.

Desert Tradition The way of life followed by the ancestors of the Pueblo Indians from around 8,000 to 300 B.C.; Desert people were nomadic and lived by hunting animals and gathering plant food but eventually learned how to grow crops.

District Six The land area immediately surrounding the 11 Hopi reservation villages that the Bureau of Indians Affairs' Hopi Indian Agency took charge of in 1943, effectively reducing the Hopi land base to only a little more than one-fifth of the reservation land that they had originally been granted.

Indian Claims Court A federal court founded in 1946 to deal with Indian land disputes.

Indian Reorganization Act (IRA) The 1934 federal law, sometimes known as the Wheeler-Howard Act, that ended the policy of allotting plots of land to individuals and encourged the development of reservation communities; the act also provided for the creation of autonomous tribal governments.

kachinas Supernatural beings associated with the spirits of ancestors, who are believed to live in mountains on the borders of Hopi territory; Hopi religion and world view is centered on maintaining the proper relationship with the kachinas.

kachinvaki The initiation rite, consisting of prayers and songs that teach about the spirit world, that Hopi children follow to become members of a kiva society.

kikmongwi A town chief who gives advice and supervises the planning of village ceremonies.

kivas Rectangular structures built completely or partially underground where Hopi meet for religious ceremonies.

lineage A group of people who claim descent from a common ancestor.

matrilineal Tracing lines of descent through the mother's lineage.

mesa A flat-topped, tablelike hill.

metates Stones for grinding seeds and nuts.

Mogollon Tradition The way of life followed by the ancestors of the Pueblo Indians from around 300 B.C. to A.D. 1100; Mogollon people transformed the culture of the Desert people by making pottery, building permanent dwellings, and learning how to plant more corps with more advanced agricultural techniques and tools.

Navajo-Hopi Settlement Act A 1974 law that divided formerly joint-use land equally between the Navajo and the Hopi.

Niman A festive dance in mid-July at which the Hopi bid farewell to the kachinas before their annual return to the spirit world.

piki The cooking stone used to make wafer-thin blue cornmeal bread, also called piki.

Progressives A group of Hopi who favored the modern style of elected representatives, in opposition to the Traditionals.

Pueblo Revolt The first and only time in history that all the Pueblo Indians acted together, the 1680 revolt had as its purpose to throw off the yoke of the Spanish; it succeeded in driving the Spanish out of New Mexico until the reconquest of 1692.

reservation A tract of land retained by Indians for their own occupation and use.

Soyal A December ritual performed to renew the earth and its life-giving forces.

Traditionals A group of Hopi who sought to maintain clan chiefs as the legitimate local leaders and uphold tribal protection of the land.

tribe A society consisting of several or many separate communities united by kinship, culture, language, and other social institutions, including clans, religious organizations, and warrior societies.

PICTURE CREDITS

NANCY BONVILLAIN is an adjunct professor at the New School for Social Research. She has a Ph.D. in anthropology from Columbia University. Dr. Bonvillain has written a grammar book and dictionary of the Mohawk language as well as *The Huron* (1989), *The Mohawk* (1992), and *Black Hawk* (1994) for Chelsea House.

FRANK W. PORTER III, general editor of INDIANS OF NORTH AMERICA, is director of the Chelsea House Foundation for American Indian Studies. He holds a B.A., M.A., and Ph.D. from the University of Maryland. He has done extensive research concerning the Indians of Maryland and Delaware and is the author of numerous articles on their history, archaeology, geography, and ethnography. He was formerly director of the Maryland Commission on Indian Affairs and American Indian Research and Resource Institute, Gettysburg, Pennsylvania, and he has received grants from the Delaware Humanities Forum, the Maryland Committee for the Humanities, the Ford Foundation, and the National Endowment for the Humanities, among others. Dr. Porter is the author of *The Bureau of Indian Affairs* in the Chelsea House KNOW YOUR GOVERNMENT series.